AF412328

Norbert Prangenberg
Paintings

Norbert Prangenberg
Paintings

KERBER ART

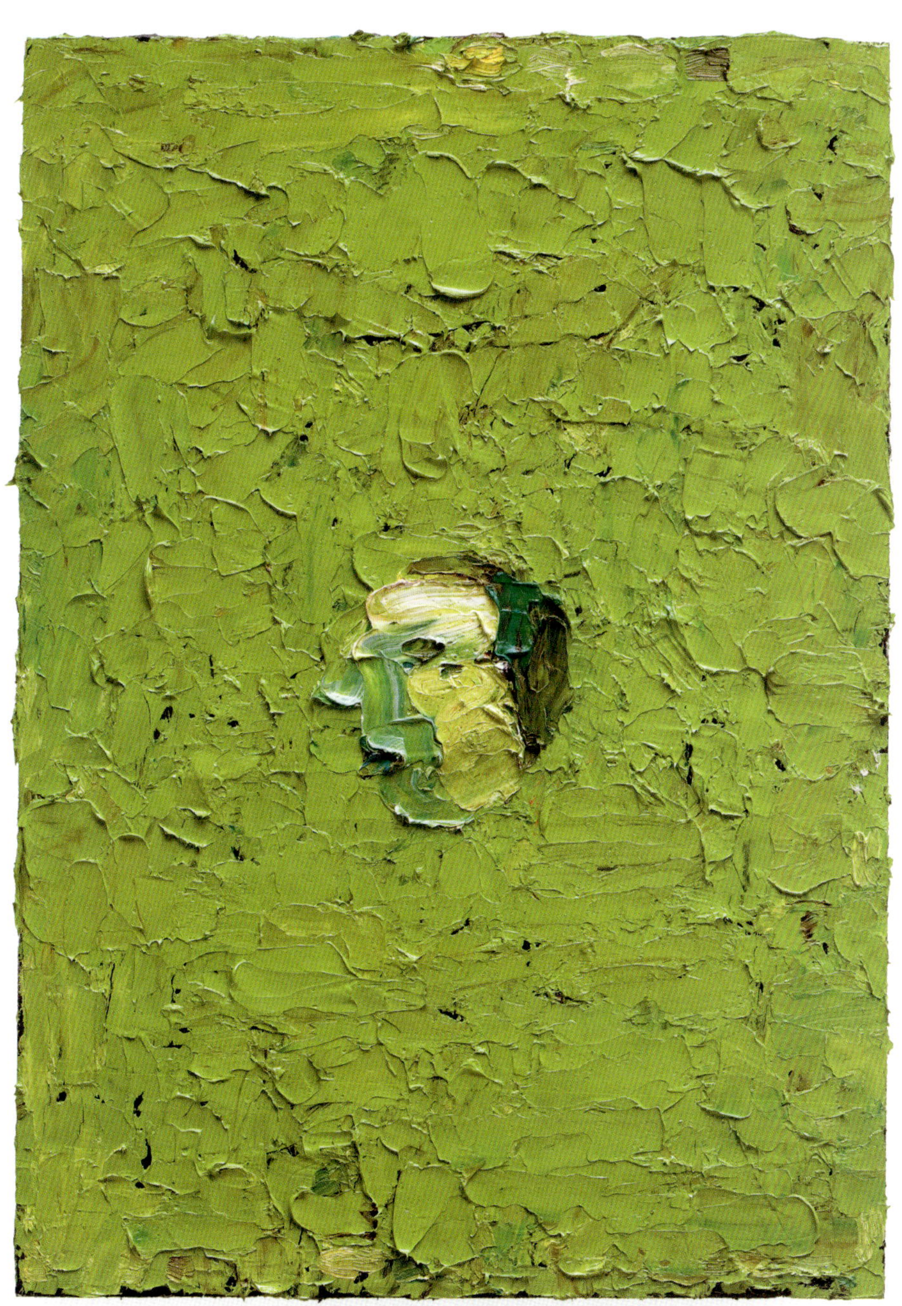

Faces

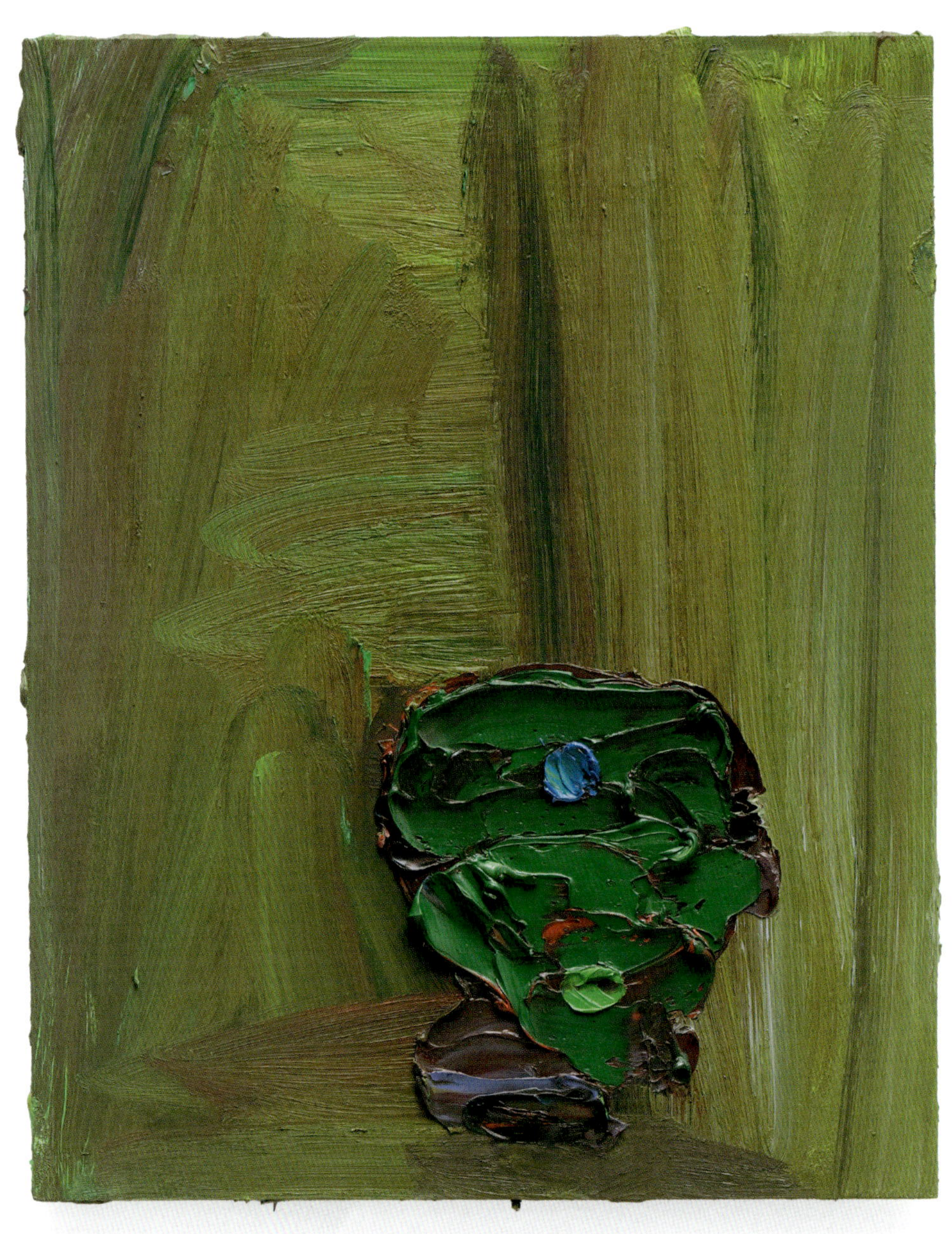

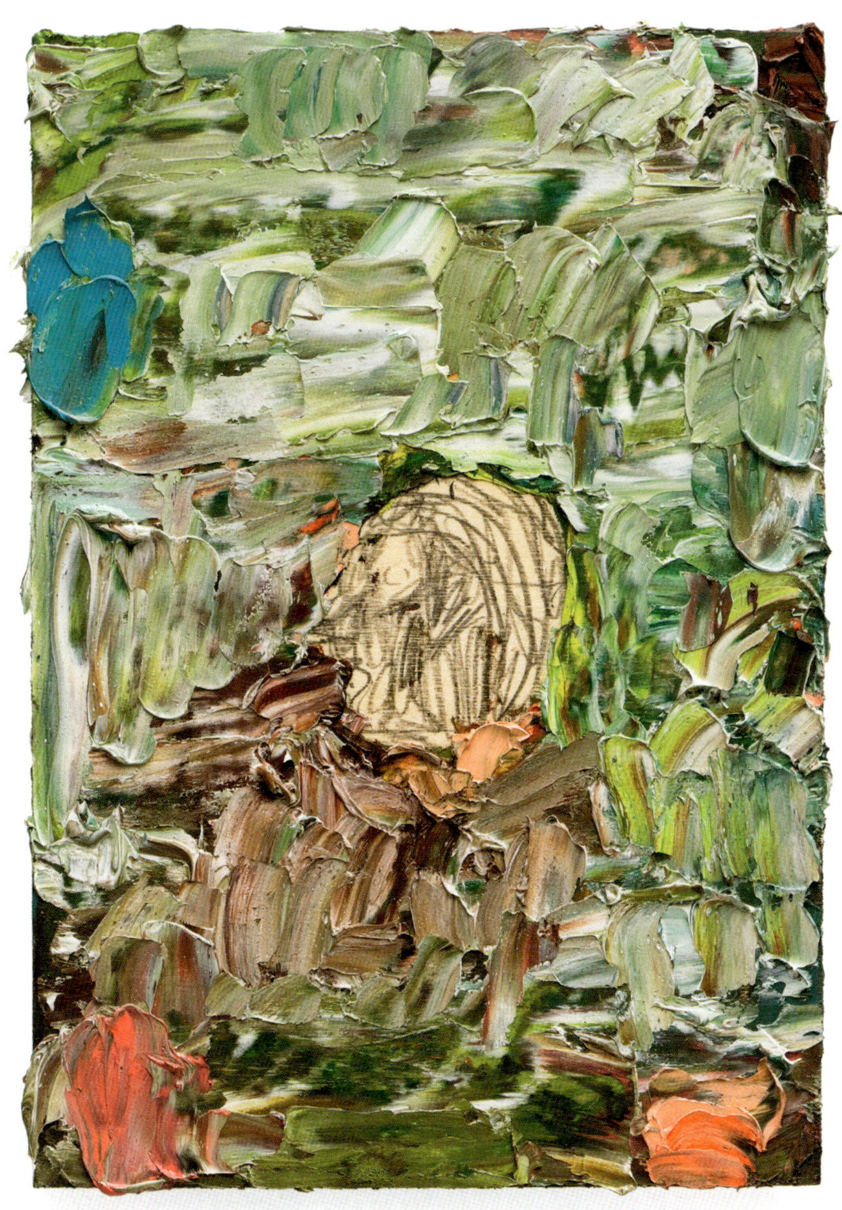

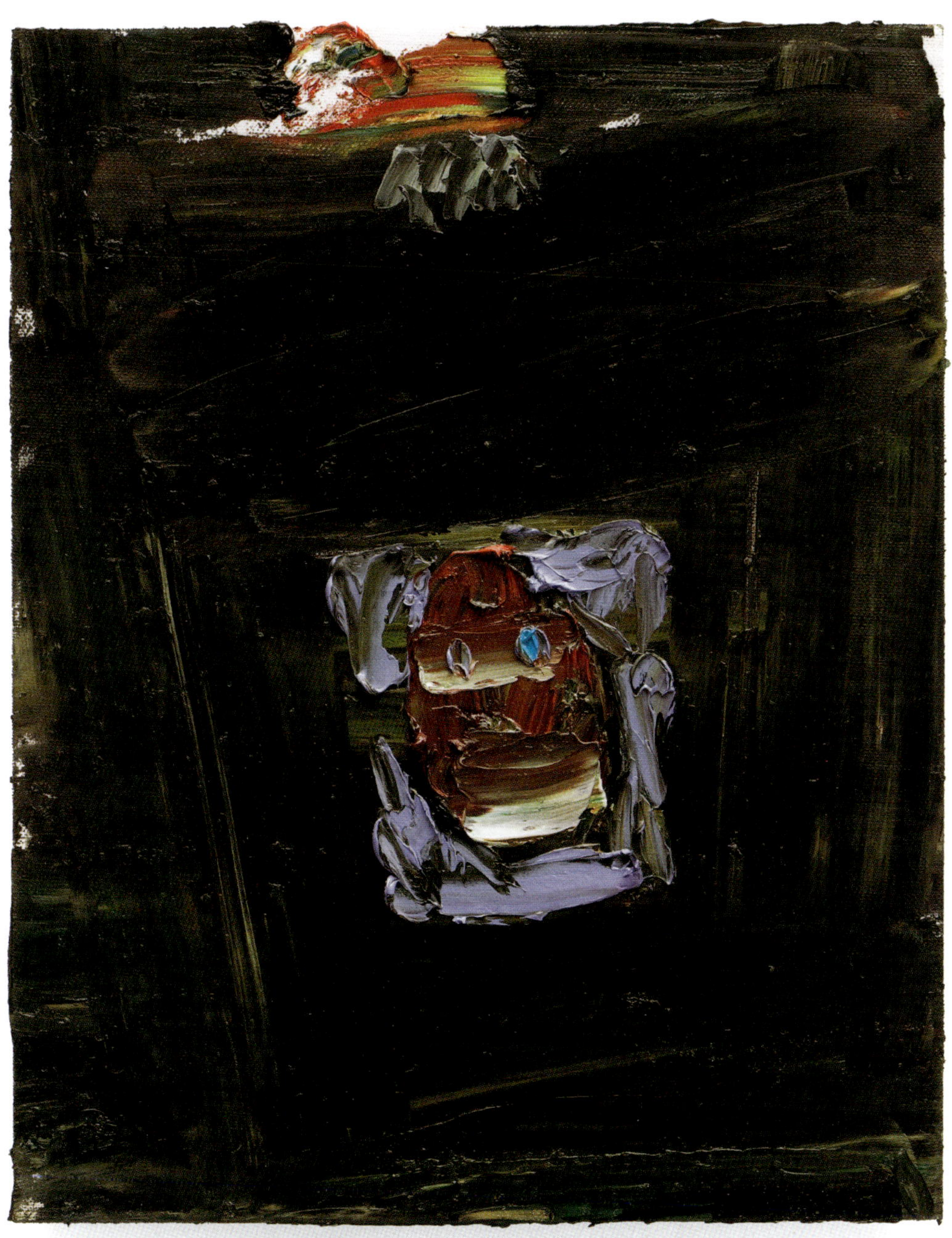

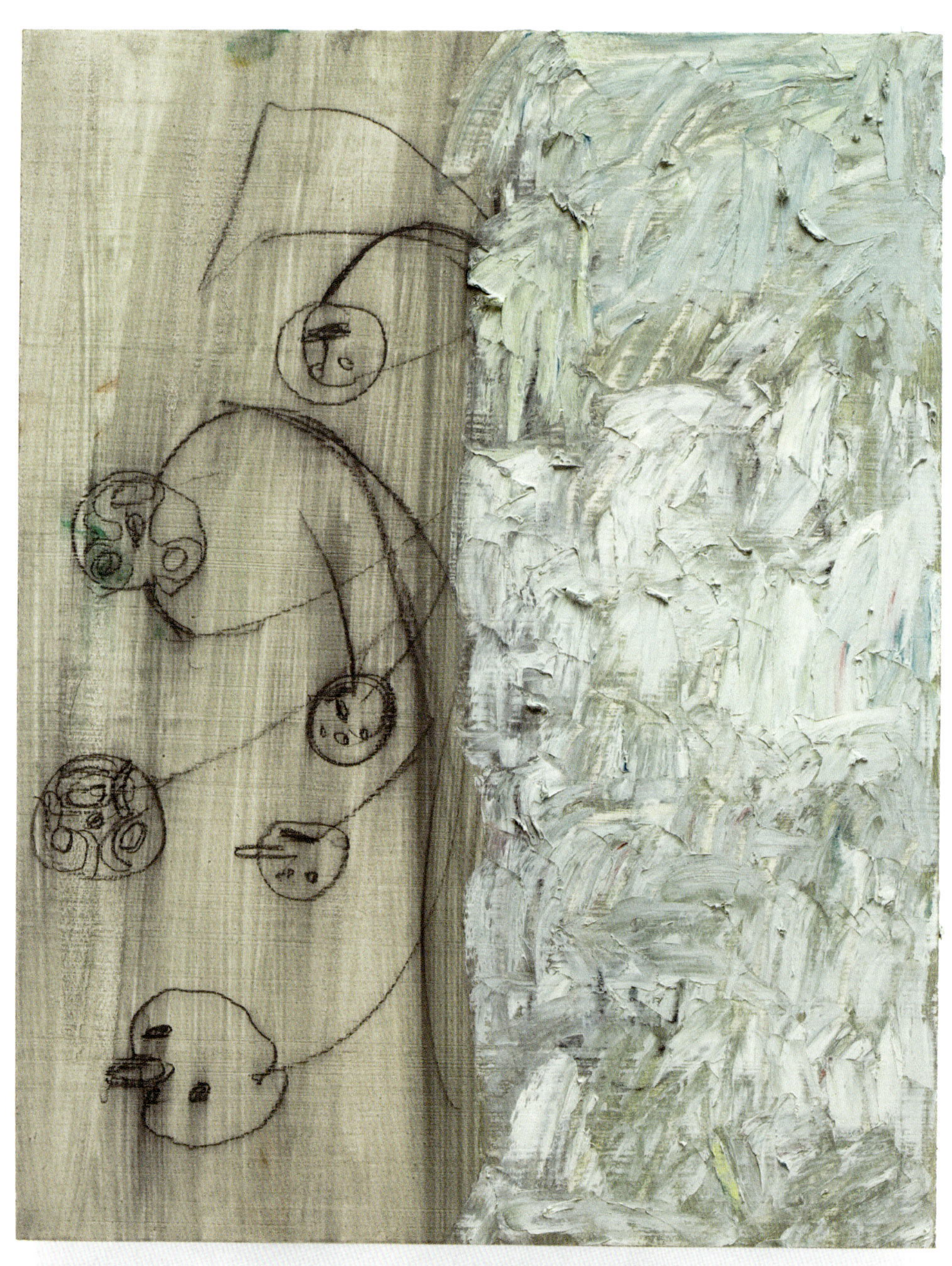

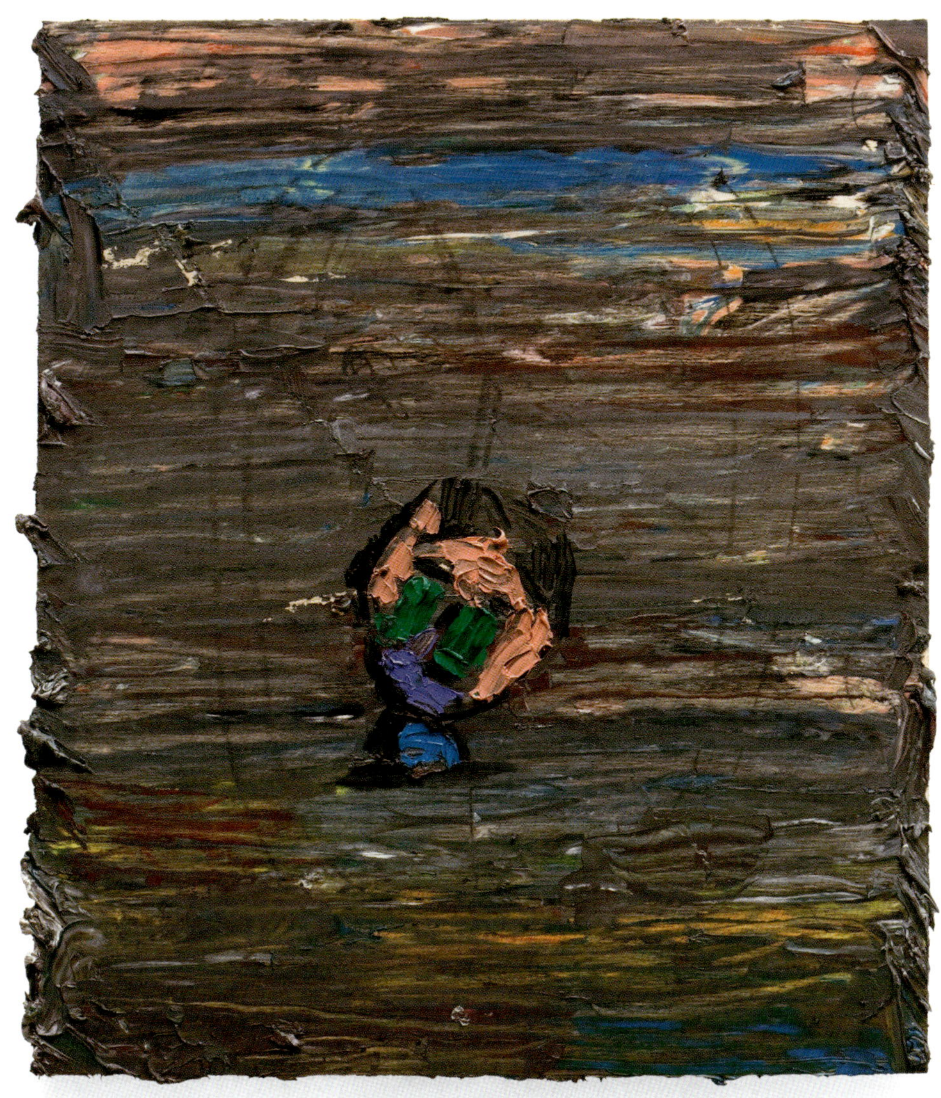

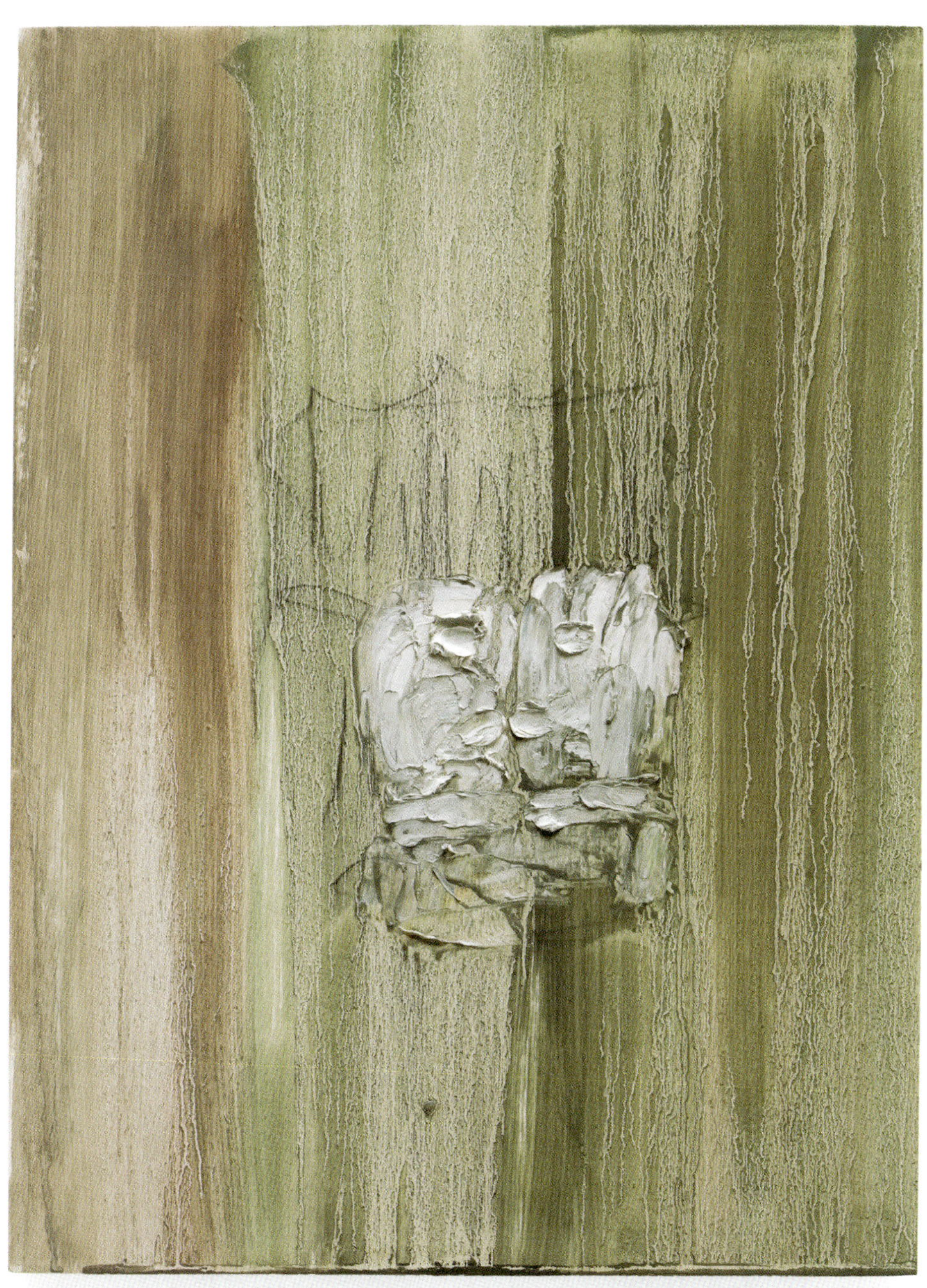

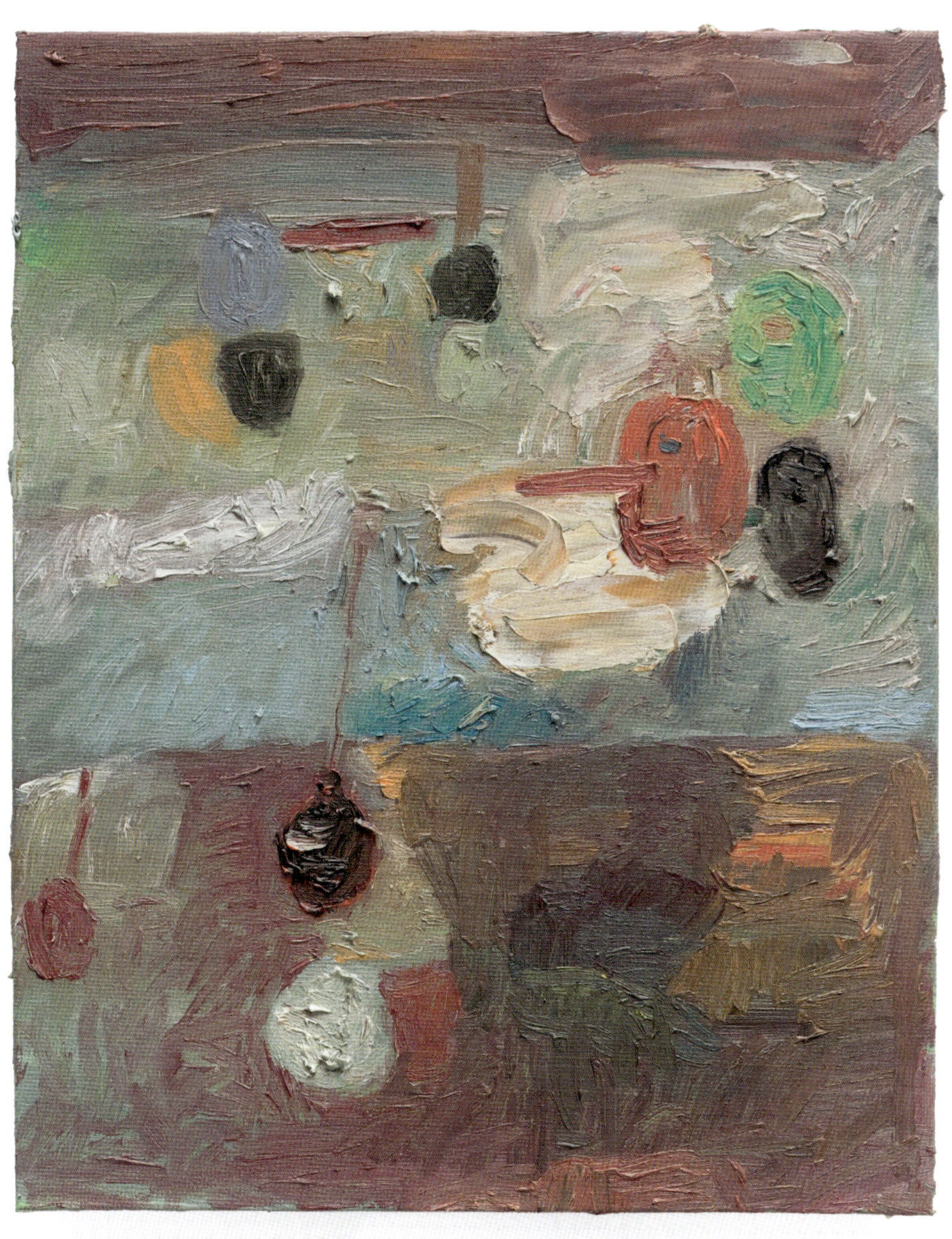

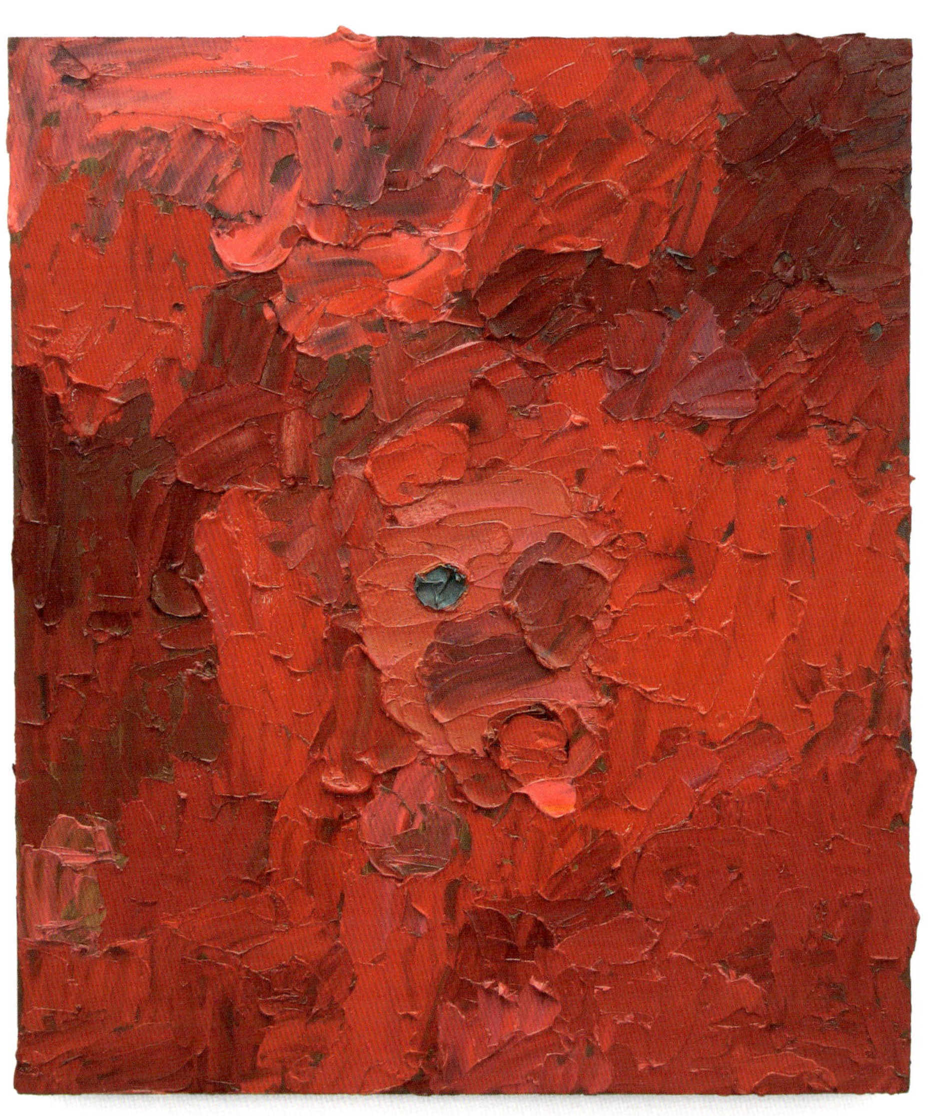

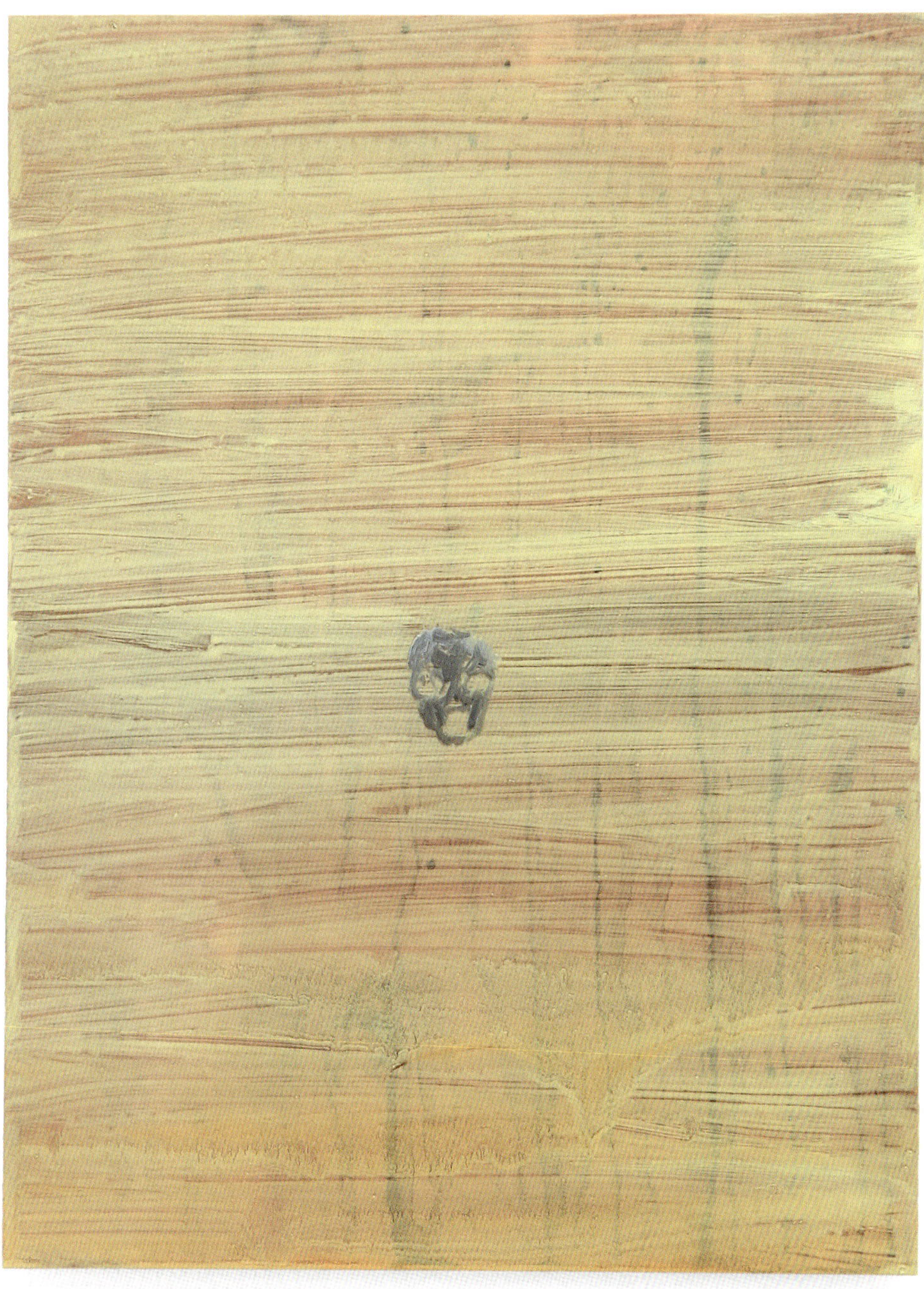

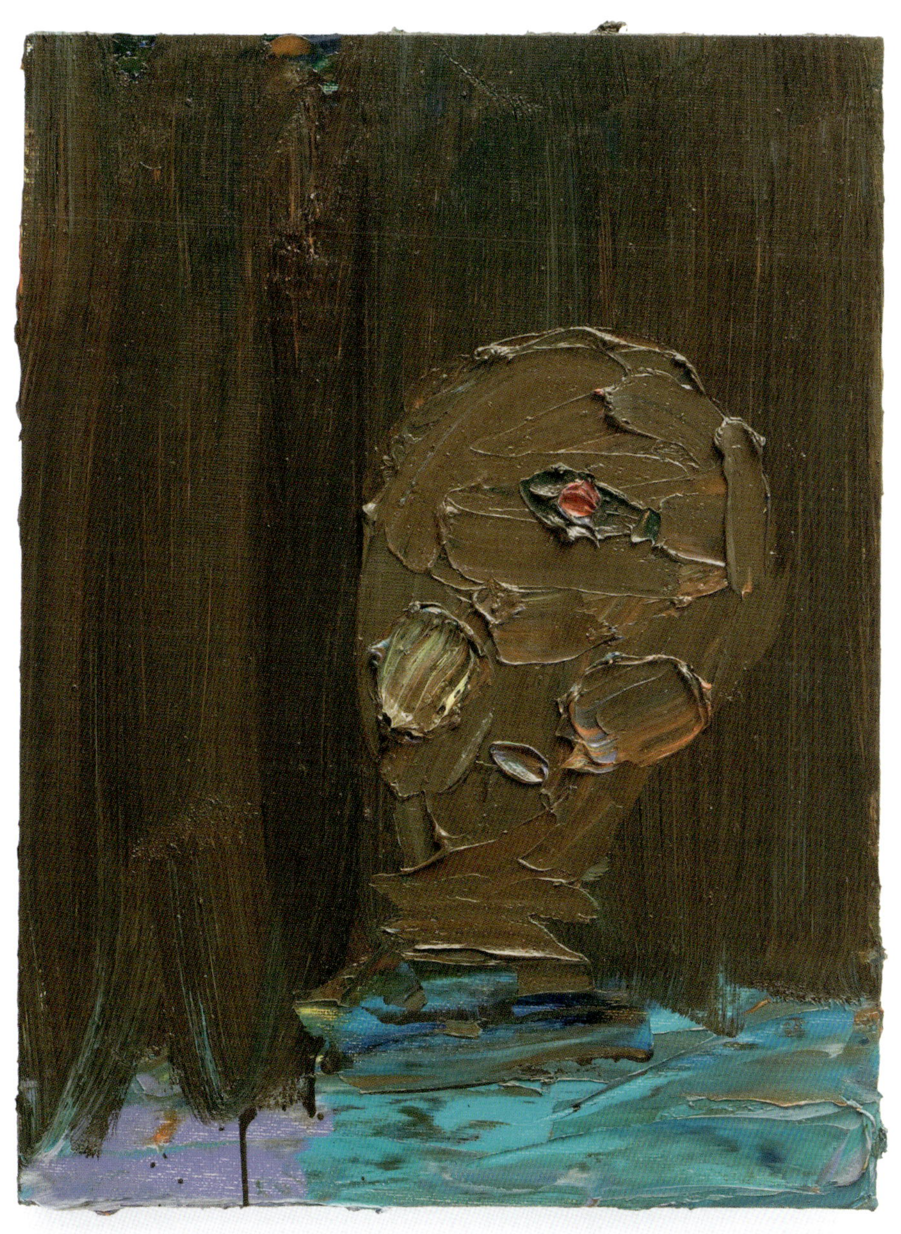

Die Aushändigung von Farbe

Theorie / Gefragt, welche Veränderungen er in der bevorstehenden Dekade für die Kunst erwarte, hat Boris Groys 2010 (im Kunstmagazin *art*) einen Bedeutungszuwachs der Theorie prophezeit. Man kann sich fragen, ob das wirklich so neu wäre. Schon zu Beginn des letzten Jahrhunderts war ja ein steiler Anstieg des Theorieaufkommens zu beobachten gewesen – man denke nur an die Manifeste, die von den Futuristen bis zu den Surrealisten die Radikalisierung der Moderne verkündeten; an die Schriften, mit denen Wassily Kandinsky seinen Weg in die Gegenstandslosigkeit begleitete; an die Überlegungen Marcel Duchamps, der bekanntlich einer der ersten Leser Kandinskys war. Schon Georges Seurat war ein theorielastiger Künstler gewesen, mit seinem kuriosen Versuch, die Malerei auf eine wissenschaftliche Grundlage zu stellen.

Ein neuer Höhepunkt in der Theoretisierung der Kunstproduktion fiel in die Zeit nach dem Zweiten Weltkrieg: In der Phase der internationalen Durchsetzung der modernen Kunst wurde gerade die Abstraktion durch die Theorieanstrengung vieler Künstler begleitet, nicht zuletzt im Umfeld des New Yorker Abstrakten Expressionismus. Aufzeichnungen und Äußerungen jener Jahre belegen einen hohen Theorieanteil in der Kunstproduktion, wie er auch für die Kunstausbildung in den USA verbindlich werden sollte und für die maßgebliche Kunstkritik, die Clement Greenberg repräsentierte. Diese Dominanz der Theorie in der Kunstproduktion hat Tom Wolfe dann zum Thema seiner Streitschrift *The Painted Word* gemacht (1975, deutsch *Das gemalte Wort. Moderne Kunst am Wendepunkt)*, ein ebenso witziges wie gescheites Buch über das *unfriendly takeover* des Handwerks durch die Theorie, das auf eine verräterisch starke Ablehnung gerade bei Kunsttheoretikern stieß.

Im Westdeutschland der Nachkriegszeit stellte sich die Lage völlig anders dar. Dort war die Phase der künstlerischen Theoriebildung eines Kandinsky, eines Paul Klee oder Johannes Itten zwar als historisches Bildungsgut präsent, aber es war – bis auf Willi Baumeister – kein Nachfolger in Sicht für eine neue Kurzstreckendogmatik; die versprengten Münchener Situationisten der Gruppe *Spur* wie die Düsseldorfer Propagandisten von *ZERO* wirkten um die Wende zu den 1960er Jahren eher wie französische Importe. Zwar beherrschte die traditionell hohe Theoriegläubigkeit der Konstruktivisten auch die *nouvelles tendances*, die erste genuin europäische Nachkriegskonstellation, und Max Bense kündigte eine verlässliche Computerästhetik an; aber beide Utopien waren schneller Geschichte, als man erwartet hätte.

Im kommunistischen Teil Deutschlands wurde dagegen eine rigide Vorherrschaft der Theorie über die Kunst durchexerziert, die es im Westen gerade auch als Freiheit erscheinen ließ, sich auf Theorien nicht einlassen zu

The 'Handing Out' of Colour

Theory / When asked (by *art* magazine in 2010) to describe the changes he expected to occur in art over the coming decade, the critic Boris Groys predicted an increase in the importance of theory. One might wonder whether this would actually be such a new development. A sharp rise in art theory could already be observed as far back as the beginning of the last century – one need only recall the manifestos of the avant-garde movements, from the Futurists to the Surrealists, which heralded the radicalisation of modernism; Wassily Kandinsky's writings on art that accompanied his forays into abstraction; or the theoretical reflections of Marcel Duchamp, who is known to have been one of the first to have read Kandinsky. Georges Seurat, too, was deeply interested in theory, as indicated by his curious attempts to place painting on a scientific basis.

The theorisation of art production reached a new peak in the period following the Second World War: at the time when modern art was asserting itself internationally, many artists – not least those associated with New York School Abstract Expressionism – sought to establish a theoretical basis for their practice, and for abstraction in particular. Notes and statements from the period confirm that theory was now a major component of art production, and this became the standard not only for fine art education in the USA, but also for the most influential body of art criticism, represented by Clement Greenberg. The dominant role played by theory in art production was also addressed by Tom Wolfe in his polemic *The Painted Word* (1975); this highly entertaining and intelligent essay on the 'unfriendly takeover' of craft by theory drew a revealingly hostile response, especially from art theorists.

It was a completely different situation in postwar West Germany, however. Here, although the formulation of artistic theories by the likes of Kandinsky, Paul Klee and Johannes Itten was an acknowledged part of historico-cultural heritage, there was – with the exception of Willi Baumeister – no sign of a successor to establish a new, short-range dogmatic; as the 1960s dawned, the expelled Situationists in the Munich-based *Spur* group and the Düsseldorf propagandists of the *ZERO* group seemed more like French imports. Although the *nouvelles tendances* – the first genuinely European postwar constellation – were dominated by the Constructivists' traditionally strong theoretical approach, and Max Bense promised a reliable theory of information aesthetics, both utopias were more rapidly consigned to history than might have been expected.

In communist East Germany, on the other hand, the rigid hegemony of theory over art was sustained, so that for those in the West, not having to concern themselves with theory also seemed like a kind of freedom – it is no coincidence that Georg Baselitz and Eugen Schönebeck, having fled the GDR, advocated a radical subjectivism in their

müssen – in ihren gemeinsamen Manifesten vertraten die DDR-Flüchtlinge Georg Baselitz und Eugen Schönebeck nicht zufällig einen radikalen Subjektivismus. Im Westdeutschland der Nachkriegszeit waren somit weder die Kunst noch die Kunstkritik oder gar der Akademieunterricht so deutlich von Theorien geprägt, wie das in den Vereinigten Staaten der Fall war.

Inzwischen hat sich freilich, nicht zuletzt im Zeichen des Poststrukturalismus, auch unter deutschen Kritikern und Kuratoren eine eifrige Kultur des Diskurses entwickelt, welche die Künstler nicht unbeeindruckt lassen konnte. Aber die erfolgreichen unter ihnen wissen natürlich, dass es längst der Markt ist, der ihr Schicksal dominiert, oft sogar bis hinein in die Form ihrer Werke. So hat jetzt einer der gefragtesten Künstler der ersten Dekade des 21. Jahrhunderts, Anselm Reyle, in der lässigen Offenheit des Erfolgs eingestanden (der *Frankfurter Allgemeinen Sonntagszeitung*), dass man „mittlerweile zwei sehr verschiedene Arten von Kunst" gleichzeitig macht: „auf der einen Seite diejenige für Galerien, Messen und Sammler, auf der anderen Seite die Kunst der Biennalen, der thematischen Ausstellungen, Kunst für den Diskurs".

Kunst für den Markt und Kunst für den Diskurs aus einer Hand – was soll angesichts dieser Polarität der Zielgruppen aus der Kunst selber werden? Gibt es sie wirklich noch als autonome Instanz oder wird sie zwischen den beiden externen Bezugsgrößen aufgerieben? Hat sie eine eigene Geltung behalten, die nicht in Diskursbegriffen und Auktionstabellen aufgeht? Angesichts der Prophezeiung von Boris Groys könnte man sich ja auch fragen, ob es überhaupt wünschenswert wäre, dass künftig die Theorie eine (noch) größere Rolle in der Kunstproduktion spielen sollte.

Handwerk / Aber wie sähe das Gegenteil aus? Das lässt sich anhand des Werkes von Norbert Prangenberg anschaulich machen, denn seine Kunst ist Handwerk im Sinn einer elementaren Interaktion von Hand, Auge und Material. Der 1949 geborene Rheinländer hat in den zahlreichen Gattungen, in denen er tätig ist, stets auf diese direkte Auseinandersetzung mit dem Material gesetzt, die eine ganz eigene Dialektik zwischen Autor und Materie in Gang setzt. Anfangs war Prangenberg noch mit Entwürfen für Glas und Edelmetalle beschäftigt, aber schon während der 1970er Jahre zogen einige Protagonisten der Düsseldorfer Akademie seine Aufmerksamkeit auf sich – Joseph Beuys und dessen Schüler Palermo sowie Reiner Ruthenbeck. Es war nicht der ausufernde Polittheoretiker Beuys, für den Prangenberg sich interessierte, sondern der empfindsame und bestechende Zeichner und Druck-grafiker Beuys, der erkennbar die Spontaneität und handschriftliche Direktheit des Informel beerbt hatte.

joint manifestos. In postwar West Germany, therefore, neither art practice nor art criticism, nor even academic art education, was as strongly influenced by theory as their equivalents were in the United States.

Since that time, of course – not least due to the emergence of post-structuralism – an avid culture of discourse has also developed among critics and curators in Germany, and this could hardly leave artists unaffected. The more successful among them are however fully aware that the art market has long since assumed control over their fate, even to the point of influencing the form of their works. For example, one of the most sought-after artists of the first decade of the 21st century, Anselm Reyle, admitted (to the *Frankfurter Allgemeine Sonntagszeitung*) with the casual frankness of success that artists nowadays produce "two very different kinds of art" at the same time: "on the one hand there is the art for galleries, art fairs and collectors, and on the other, the art to be shown at Biennials and in thematic exhibitions – art for the discourse". Art for the market and art for the discourse, created by a single hand – given this polarity between its target audiences, what is to become of art? Does it still exist as an autonomous entity or is it worn away by the friction between the two external frames of reference? Has it retained its own validity, one that is not incorporated into discourse-related concepts and auction charts? In the light of Boris Groys' prediction, one might wonder just how desirable it is for theory to play an (even) greater role in art production.

Craft / But what would the opposite scenario be? It can perhaps be illustrated with reference to the work of Norbert Prangenberg, as his art is craftsmanship in the sense of a fundamental interaction between hand, eye and material. Working within numerous genres, he invariably favours this kind of direct engagement, which initiates a very specific dialectic between an author and his material. Born in the Rhineland in 1949, Prangenberg began his career creating works in glass and precious metals, but by the 1970s his attention was already being drawn to some of the leading figures at the Düsseldorf Art Academy – Joseph Beuys and his pupils Palermo and Reiner Ruthenbeck. Prangenberg was less interested in Beuys as an expansive political theorist than as a sensitive and impressive draughtsman and printmaker who had clearly inherited the spontaneity and graphic immediacy of Art Informel.

A recommendation by Mönchengladbach museum director Johannes Cladders led to Prangenberg's first exhibitions at Haus Esters in Krefeld and at Karsten Greve's gallery in Cologne, and in 1982 Prangenberg was already among those taking part in *documenta 7*. The works he showed in Kassel were sculptures made of paper, concrete and pigment, along with a number of large-scale drawings; these reflected only two facets of his diverse practice, in which painting already played a major part.

Eine Empfehlung des Mönchengladbacher Museumsleiters Johannes Cladders führte zu ersten Ausstellungen Prangenbergs im Haus Esters in Krefeld sowie in der Kölner Galerie von Karsten Greve, und schon 1982 gehörte Prangenberg zu den Teilnehmern der *documenta 7*. In Kassel zeigte er Plastiken aus Papier, Beton und Pigment sowie großformatige Zeichnungsblätter; sie repräsentierten freilich nur zwei der vielen Arbeitsweisen von Prangenberg, zu denen maßgeblich auch schon die Malerei zählte.

In seiner Malerei ging es damals um meist großflächige Bilder, die aus Pastell, Pigment, Öl und Wasserfarben auf Papieren oder Leinwänden gleichsam *geschöpft* wurden: Die Bildträger lagen auf dem Boden und Zufallsverläufe des Wassers sowie Absetzbewegungen der Pigmente spielten ebenso in die Gestalt hinein wie markant gesetzte Zeichen. Diese „Bilder" genannten Malereien entstanden in einer manchmal gelassenen, manchmal raschen Interaktion mit dem Material, bei der Entscheidungen zu fällen waren, die sich nicht nach irgendeiner Theorie hätten ausrichten lassen, sondern, je nach Lage der Dinge auf der Leinwand oder auf dem Papier, im Prozess zu treffen waren.

Daneben bilden Holzdrucke, Linolschnitte und Lithografien weitere Arbeitsschwerpunkte dieses Künstlers, lyrisch anmutende Farbflächen und Umrissformen, die nicht zufällig von Dichtern gerne als kongeniale Illustrationen ihrer Bücher verwendet worden sind. Inzwischen hat Norbert Prangenberg an der Münchner Akademie, wo er 1993 zum Professor ernannt wurde, neben der Meisterklasse für Keramik auch die für Glas übernommen, und damit rundet sich das Bild der vielen Gattungen, in denen er tätig ist, auch biografisch ab.

Vokabular ohne Erzählung / Es macht die Besonderheit des Werkes von Prangenberg aus, dass er in all diesen Gattungen dieselbe Handschrift hat. Denn es ist stets das lebendige Zusammenwirken von Hand, Material und Auge, das ihn interessiert und dem er in einer souveränen Mischung aus lustvoller Arbeit und ernsthaftem Spiel nachgeht. Dabei bringt er die zeichenhaft wirkenden Verweise in geometrischer Knappheit ein – Kreis, Quadrat, Trapez, Rhombus, Oval oder Dreieck; breite Schlangenlinien, schmale Zackenleisten, irreguläre Spiralen oder konzentrische Wellenkonturen, die wie ein gattungsübergreifendes Vokabular erscheinen, aus dem sich aber keine Erzählung ergibt.

Die Zeichen aus diesem Inventar tauchen in den verschiedenen Gattungen auf, haben dort aber unterschiedliche Wirkungen: In den frühen Pastell- und Pigmentmalereien schimmern die Formen durch halbopake Farbsedimente, als ob sie dem Bild einen Start hätten geben sollen, damit es sich, von ihnen abstoßend, frei entwickeln

At that time, Prangenberg's paintings were mainly expansive images that were 'scooped' out of pastel, pigment, oil and watercolour onto paper or canvas: the supports were laid on the ground, so that the random motion of the water and the way the pigments then settled on the surface played as much of a role in creating the composition as did the artist's distinctly placed marks. Entitled "Bilder" (pictures), these paintings were created through direct interaction with the material – a sometimes leisurely, sometimes rapid process requiring decisions to be made that could not have been aligned with some theory or other but instead had to be made during the process itself, in response to the particular situation occurring on the canvas or paper. In addition to this painting technique, Prangenberg used woodcut, linocut and lithography to create lyrical colour planes and contoured forms, and it is no coincidence that these images are often chosen by poets as fittingly expressive illustrations for their publications. Having been appointed professor at the Academy of Fine Arts in Munich in 1993, Norbert Prangenberg now teaches the master class in glass as well as that in ceramics, thereby rounding off the biographical image of his diverse artistic practice.

Vocabulary without narrative / What makes Prangenberg's work stand out is that he retains his signature style in all of these different genres. His overriding interest is in exploring the lively interplay of hand, eye and material, which he does by confidently combining enjoyable labour with serious playfulness. Emblematic references are introduced with geometric conciseness – circle, square, trapezium, rhombus, oval or triangle – while broad wavy lines, narrow serrated strips, irregular spirals and concentric waves seem to form a genre-transcending vocabulary, but one that does not yield a narrative.

The symbols from this inventory appear in all the various genres, but to different effect in each context: in the early pastel and pigment paintings, the forms shine through semi-opaque colour sediments as if they were intended to start the picture off – enabling it to then detach itself and develop a life of its own – or to give the viewer something to hold on to, some kind of orientation in the cloudy colour transitions. In the prints, on the other hand, such forms are set onto the paper with clearly defined contours like heraldic emblems of abstraction – distinct or playful, decorative or enigmatic, they are always in a state of suspense, as if giving notice of a forthcoming communication that ultimately fails to arrive; sometimes they recall the clefs for a piece of music that cannot be noted down. In the drawings, these abbreviated symbols assume an independent existence as direct inscriptions in the artist's hand, while the ceramic sculptures wear the forms like body jewellery – covered with liquid glaze, decorated with

konnte, oder dem Betrachter einen Halt, um sich in den wolkigen Farbübergängen zu orientieren. In der Druckgrafik sind solche Formen dagegen klar konturiert auf das Papier gesetzt, wie eine Heraldik der Abstraktion, markant oder verspielt, dekorativ oder verrätselt, und immer in der Schwebe einer angekündigten Mitteilung, die ausbleibt – bisweilen wirken sie wie Notenschlüssel für eine Musik, die sich nicht aufzeichnen lässt. In den Zeichnungen schließlich entwickeln diese Kürzel ein Eigenleben der direkten Handschrift, und die keramischen Plastiken tragen sie wie einen Körperschmuck – mit flächendeckender Glasur überschüttet, mit schartigen Narben versehen oder mit verinselten Spielräumen der Farbe.

So ist in rund drei Jahrzehnten ein breit gelagertes Œuvre entstanden, eines, das Bildhauerei wie Malerei, Zeichnung und Druckgrafik in einer organischen Handschrift zusammenfasst, wie man es angesichts der verschiedenen Herausforderungen der gattungscharakteristischen Materialien nicht leicht für möglich halten würde.

Motorik / Der Handschrift liegt eine forschende Motorik zugrunde, mit der sich Prangenberg durch sein Œuvre bewegt, ohne einer der verschiedenen Gattungen auf Dauer den Vorzug zu geben, aber auch ohne der einen die materiellen Gesetze der anderen überzustülpen. Man hätte eine solche Vorgehensweise in der Apologetik der Nachkriegszeit vermutlich als experimentell bezeichnet, aber sie ist forciert spielerisch, ebenso neugierig wie geduldig, mit Formen und Farben gerüstet, ohne diese in die Galeerensklaverei einer ästhetischen Programmatik zu zwingen.

Diese Motorik des Handwerks folgt einer eigenen *Theatralität des Kunstmachens,* wie sie sich neben dem Abstrakten Expressionismus auch bei seinen europäischen Äquivalenten, Informel und Tachismus, entwickelt und zugespitzt hatte. Man kann das vielleicht am besten an den Übertreibungen veranschaulichen – an den eleganten Exzessen eines Georges Mathieu, der sich unter freiem Himmel in Szene setzte, um das spontane Herbeipinseln seiner Bilder dem Publikum sowie vor allem den Fotografen und Filmemachern vorzuführen; an Yves Klein, der seine Aktabdrücke in einer koketten Performance direkt vor dem Galeriepublikum entstehen ließ; an Günter Brus, der aus der gestischen Aktion vor der Leinwand in die Gestik seiner heute noch atemberaubend radikalen Performances des Wiener Aktionismus fand.

Die Theatralität des Kunstmachens war aber schon vor diesen Zuspitzungen ein prominentes Medienthema der Nachkriegszeit gewesen – etwa als Pablo Picasso 1949 für die Kamera des Fotografen Gjon Mili mit einer Taschenlampe Figuren ins Dunkle zeichnete, oder als wenig später Hans Namuth seine berühmt gewordenen Filmaufnahmen davon machte, wie Jackson Pollock malte. Pollocks Action-Painting war eine forcierte Fassung jener

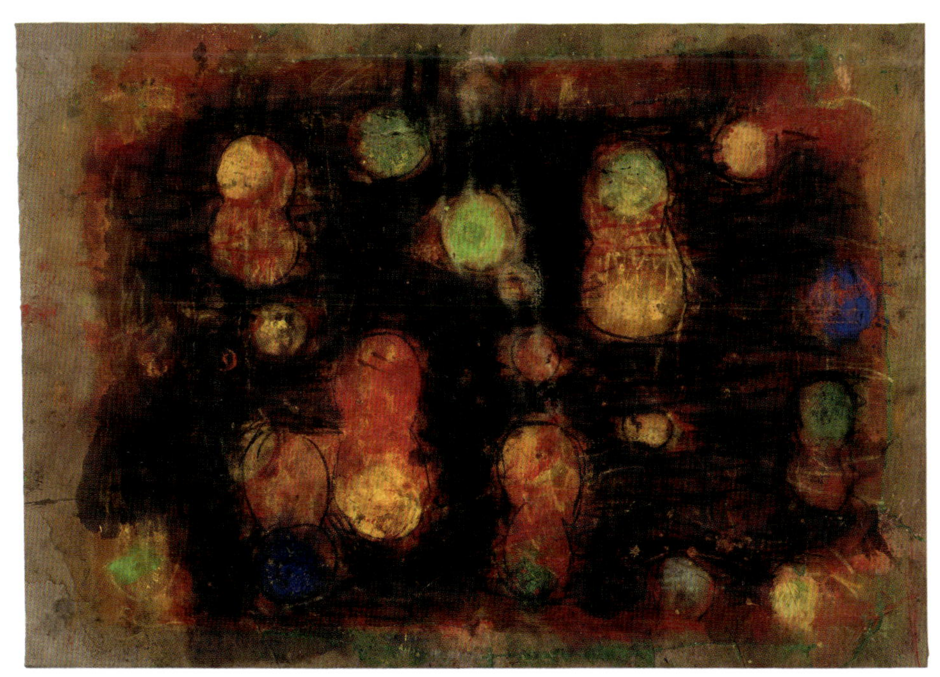

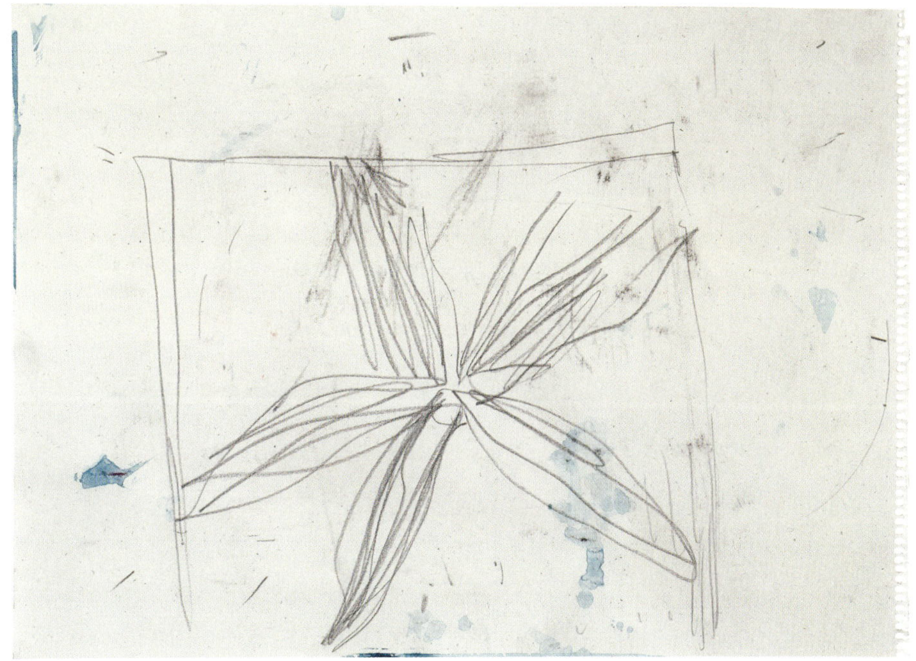

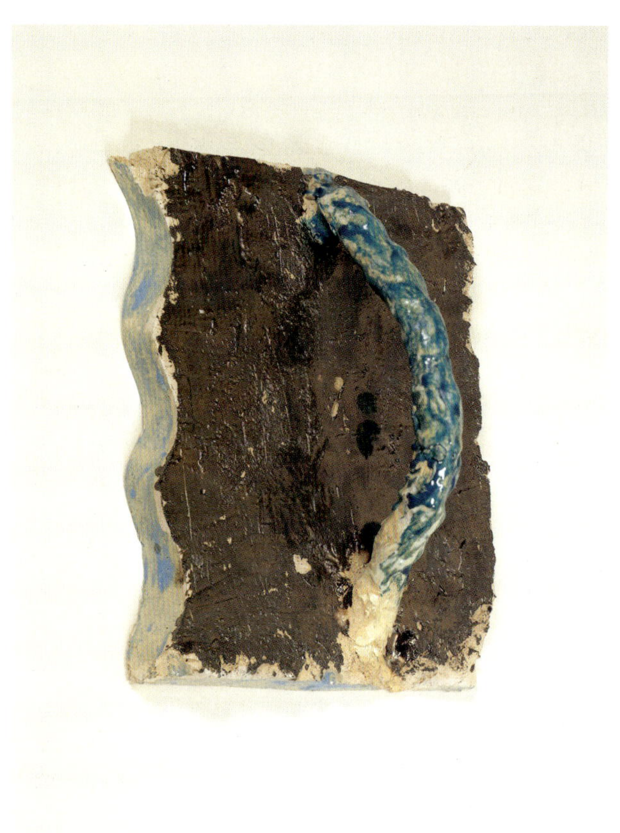

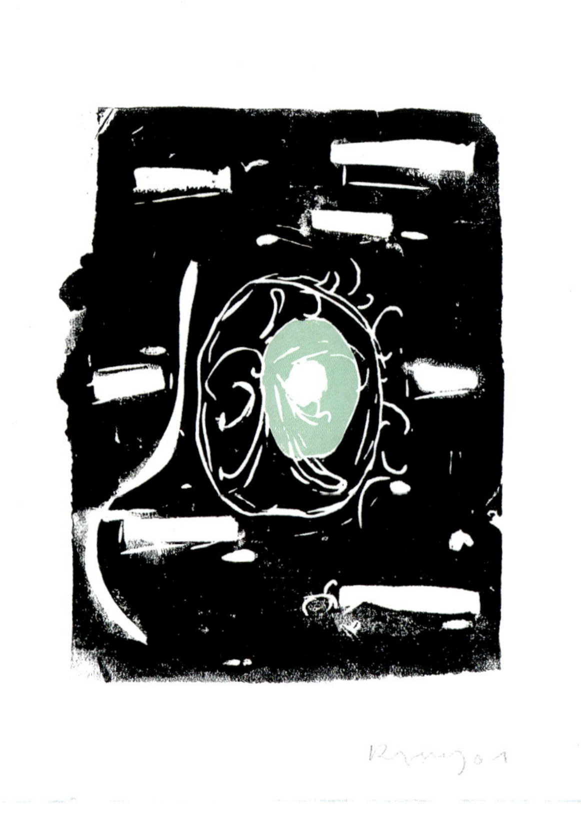

jagged scars or enriched with isolated splashes of colour. Over a period of around three decades, Prangenberg has thus created a richly varied body of work, bringing together sculpture, painting, drawing and printmaking with an organic signature style, in a way that would not normally be considered possible given the varying demands of the genre-typical materials.

Motor activity / Underlying Prangenberg's signature style is an exploratory mode of motor activity that allows him to navigate though his oeuvre without giving precedence to one of the different genres for any length of time, but also without applying the material laws of one to the others. In the apologetics of the postwar era, this kind of approach would probably have been termed experimental, but Prangenberg's method is actively playful, both curious and patient, and is armed with a wide range of forms and colours, yet without making them slaves to an aesthetic agenda.

This motor aspect of artistic craft invokes a *theatricality of art-making* similar to that which developed and was brought to a head not only in Abstract Expressionism but also in its European equivalents – Art Informel and *Tachisme.* It can perhaps best be illustrated by its exaggerated manifestations – in the elegant excesses of Georges Mathieu, for example, who staged outdoor events to demonstrate the spontaneous execution of his paintings to the viewing public, but also and above all to photographers and filmmakers; in Yves Klein's coquettish performance where nude body prints were created directly in front of a gallery audience; or in the art of Günter Brus, who proceeded from gestural expression on canvas to the explosive gesturalism of his still breathtakingly radical performances of Viennese Actionism.

Even prior to these spectacular events, however, the theatrical dimension of art-making was a popular media topic in the postwar era – for example in 1949, when Pablo Picasso drew figures with the beam of a torch inside a dark room, captured by the photographer Gjon Mili or, not long after that, when Hans Namuth made his famous film recordings of Jackson Pollock painting. Pollock's action painting was an intensified version of the motor activity that normally takes place in the studio rather than in staged appearances before the media, something Yves Klein and Georges Mathieu were certainly very good at.

In the artist's studio, the theatrics of art-making is not usually aimed at spectators – in other words, at witnesses to the process – but at those who will view the results. The work performed in the studio involves a concentrated and undisturbed interaction of material, hand and eye in a momentary situation where theories are of

Motorik, deren Schauplatz normalerweise das Atelier ist und nicht der Medienauftritt, den Yves Klein und Georges Mathieu zweifellos gut beherrschten.

Im Atelier ist die Theatralik des Kunstmachens in der Regel nicht auf Zuschauer aus, auf Zeugen des Prozesses, sondern auf Betrachter der Ergebnisse. Im Atelier geht es um das konzentrierte und ungestörte Zusammenspiel von Material, Hand und Auge in einem Moment, in dem Theorien nicht helfen und den sie letztlich auch nicht völlig erklären oder überhaupt erreichen können. In diesem Moment handelt der Künstler in einer verinnerlichten Tradition des Sehens und Machens, in der er sich als Individuum behaupten muss, will er als Künstler ernstgenommen werden, und bei dem die Ergebnisse neu sein müssen, sollen sie wahrgenommen werden.

Öl / In einer weiteren Wendung seiner Neugierde hat Prangenberg sich seit einigen Jahren in ein Material eingearbeitet, das, obwohl traditionell, nie in sein Repertoire gehört hatte: in die Ölmalerei. Zuerst lange und diskret im Atelier erprobt, bevor 2007 erste Beispiele in der Hamburger Produzentengalerie ausgestellt wurden, markieren die kleinformatigen Bilder nun eine völlig neue Werkgruppe. Ein weiteres Mal lässt sie seine Arbeitsweise als die eines sich in das Material vortastenden Handwerks erkennen.

Gerade weil die Malerei mit Öl so langwierig ist – träger als das Spiel mit in Wassern aufgelösten und verwirbelten Pigmenten; widerspenstiger als das Abreiben der Pastellkreiden; zäher als das Einkerben von Furchen und Schrunden in den nassen Ton; langsamer im Trocknen als jedes Aquarell; zeitaufwendiger im Herausarbeiten von Formen als eine Zeichnung; schließlich weniger flexibel als selbst ein Holzstock oder das Linoleum, die man nachschneiden kann – hatte die Ölmalerei ihn nie interessiert, obwohl sie jahrhundertelang der Königsweg der Malerei gewesen war.

Erst als Prangenberg sich ganz sicher war, dass er auch aus diesem Material seine variantenreiche, aber charakteristische Handschrift herausholen konnte - sei es mit dem Pinsel, dem Spachtel oder tatsächlich mit der Hand –, hat er sich auf eine erste Werkserie eingelassen. Sie war rein abstrakt und ließ keine erzählerischen Figurationen erkennen, die über die Mitteilungen des Materials von seiner Bearbeitung hinausgegangen wäre - reich orchestriert im Spiel von Farbe und Struktur, von pastosem und flächigem Auftrag, von kantigen oder schlierigen Spuren. Auch abstrakte Bilder haben ja ein Thema - die Farbe sowie die Form, in die man sie bringt – und das war das Leitmotiv der ersten Serie von Ölbildern, in denen Prangenberg der Frage nachging, „wie man Farbe malen kann". In seiner frühen Malerei mit Pigmenten und Pastellkreiden hatte Prangenberg sich schon auf die Bereitschaft

no help – a moment, ultimately, which they can never fully explain or truly grasp. At this moment, the artist is acting within an internalised tradition of seeing and making, where he must assert himself as an individual in order to be taken seriously as an artist, and where the results must be new if they are to be taken notice of at all.

Oil / Providing further indication of his artistic curiosity, for the last few years Norbert Prangenberg has been exploring a material which, although traditional, had never been part of his individual repertoire – oil paint. Following a lengthy period of discreet testing in the studio, he presented the first examples at the Produzentengalerie Hamburg in 2007, and now his small-scale oil paintings represent a completely new body of work. Here, too, his method is revealed as that of the craftsman feeling his way into the material.

It was precisely because oil painting is such a protracted process – less active than experimenting with swirling, water-soluble pigments; less controllable than rubbing pastels; tougher than cutting channels and grooves into wet clay; slower to dry than any watercolour; more time-consuming than a drawing as far as the elaboration of forms is concerned; and finally, less flexible even than a woodblock or piece of linoleum that can be recut – that oil painting had previously never interested Prangenberg, even though it had been the gold standard in painting for centuries.

Only once Prangenberg was certain that he could use this material to convey his diverse yet distinctive style – whether with the aid of a paintbrush, a spatula or simply his own hand – did he produce a first series of works. They were purely abstract, with no hint of narrative figuration beyond what the material communicated about its handling – a richly orchestrated interplay of colour and structure, impasto textures and flat surfaces, angular and streaky traces. Even abstract images have subject matter – colour and the form into which it is brought – and this was the leitmotif of Prangenberg's first series of oil paintings, in which he addressed the issue of "how to paint colour".

In his early paintings using pigments and pastels, Prangenberg had already relied – as, for example, Sigmar Polke also did in his chemical experiments with colour – on the willingness of the material to collaborate, on the innovative potential it reveals when given enough scope, and on its accommodating and cooperative generosity: if one manages not to scare colour off with theory, one can evidently enlist it as a co-creator.

Reading the clouds / A new realm has recently opened up within this interaction between author and material, as Prangenberg is now also exploring the figurative associations that emerge from the process of producing his small oil panels. What was described by Heinrich von Kleist almost exactly two hundred years ago as *The Gradual*

des Materials zur Mitarbeit verlassen – wie auch ein Sigmar Polke sie in seinen farbchemischen Anordnungen voraussetzt –, auf die Innovationslust der Materie, die sich einstellt, wenn man ihr einen Spielraum eröffnet, auf ihr Entgegenkommen und ihre kooperative Großzügigkeit: Wenn man die Farbe nicht mit Theorie abschreckt, kann man sie offenbar als Mitspieler gewinnen.

Wolkenlesen / In dieser Interaktion zwischen Autor und Material hat sich seit Kurzem ein neuer Spielraum eröffnet, weil Prangenberg nun auch den figürlichen Assoziationen nachgeht, die sich im Prozess der Verfertigung seiner kleinen Öltafeln ergeben. Was Heinrich von Kleist vor ziemlich genau zweihundert Jahren als die *Allmähliche Verfertigung der Gedanken beim Reden* festgehalten hat, bekommt bei der allmählichen Verfertigung der Bilder beim Malen einen anderen Sinn: In den Strukturen und Verwerfungen eines abstrakten Bildes werden im Machen Anflüge einer Figuration sichtbar, die nur wenig Nachhilfe braucht, damit sich die Figuren dann auch herauszuschälen, um, so Prangenberg, als „Kontrapunkt" für die ansonsten rein malerische Handhabung von Farbe und Struktur stehen bleiben zu können.

Wie es den Romantikern als ästhetischer Genuss vorkam, in den Wolken zu lesen, um flüchtige Figuren zu erkennen und ihre Formationen mit Fantasien zu bevölkern, so ist Prangenberg Linien und Knoten in der Materie nachgegangen, die sich während des Malens ergeben und Figuren nahelegen, die nun skizzenhaft aus der Struktur herausgehoben und stehengelassen werden. Jetzt geht es nicht mehr nur um *Farbe und Struktur*, sondern auch um *Motiv und Titel*.

In dieser zweiten Werkgruppe der neuen Ölbilder kehrt ein Arbeitsprinzip wieder, das schon in den Oberflächen der großen keramischen Gefäße zu erkennen war sowie in den Kleinplastiken: Dort heben sich kleine und intensive Farbzonen vom Hintergrund des offenporig belassenen keramischen Materials oder einer monochromen Glasur gleichsam insulär ab. Solche Inseln sind auch in die Ölbilder gewandert, aber dort haben sie eine andere Präsenz: Als kleine Bildzonen eigener Prägnanz kontrastieren sie die großen Bilder, von denen sie beherbergt werden. Wie Zitate abstrakter Kunstwerke markieren sie in den Gemälden eine Brechung des handwerklichen Impulses; als Bild im Bild signalisieren sie das Gedächtnis einer spontanen Vorgehensweise, die ihre eigene Geschichtlichkeit durchaus kennt.

Theorie der Praxis / Nun könnten die unermüdlichen Diskursifizierer der Kunst einwenden, ein Rückzug auf das Handwerk und seine Abenteuer sei selber eine Theorie, schlimmer noch: romantische Ideologie. In der Tat gibt es in der Kunst nichts Untheoretisches, denn im scheinbar direkten Umgang mit der Farbe sind so viele historische

Production of Thoughts Whilst Speaking takes on a new meaning in the gradual production of images whilst painting: during the process of making an abstract painting, figurative traces may also become visible in its structures and cracks, so that it requires little extra assistance for these figures to emerge and, to quote Prangenberg, provide a "counterpoint" to the otherwise purely painterly exploration of colour and structure.

Just as the Romantics found aesthetic pleasure in reading clouds, discerning fleeting shapes within their formations and populating them with figures from their imagination, so Prangenberg has pursued lines and knots that form in the material during the painting process and are suggestive of figures; he then sketchily lifts these figures out of the structure and allows them to stand out. Now it is no longer just a matter of *colour and structure*, it is also about *motif and title.*

In this second new series of oil paintings, a creative method is employed that is also apparent in the surfaces of Prangenberg's large ceramic vessels and small-scale sculptures, where small areas of intense colour stand out like islands against a background of open-pore ceramic material or monochrome glaze. Such islands have also found their way into the oil paintings, but here they have a different presence: as small but highly incisive pictorial zones they form a contrast to the large paintings in which they are contained; like quotations of abstract artworks they represent a departure from the craft impulse within the paintings; and as pictures within pictures they evoke the memory of a spontaneous method that is fully aware of its own historicity.

Theory of practice / Those who tirelessly seek to 'discursify' art may of course argue that a return to craftsmanship and its adventures is itself a theory or, worse still, a romantic ideology. Of course it is true that in art, nothing is 'untheoretical', because the seemingly direct engagement with paint involves so many historical assumptions of a technical, chemical or aesthetic nature that the act of painting ends up being mediated through multiple filters – even if the protagonists are unaware of this or unwilling to acknowledge it. Paint has such a long history of use that it can no longer offer simplicity.

As far as artistic craft is concerned, however, simplicity is not the issue at all. That impression can only be sustained if one forgets how complex handcrafted things can be and how basic, by contrast, the intellectual creations often are that can be unambiguously, completely and exhaustively translated into language. On the other hand, an art that involves physically manipulating and shaping a material – whether it is clay, linoleum, wood or a paint substance – in the attempt to produce something more than just a battle of material or mere illustration,

Voraussetzungen, technische, chemische wie ästhetische gegeben, dass es auf eine vielfach vermittelte Tätigkeit hinausläuft – selbst wenn es den Akteuren nicht bewusst sein sollte oder sie nichts davon wissen wollen. Die Farbe hat eine so lange Gebrauchsgeschichte, dass das Einfache in ihr nicht mehr vorgesehen sein kann.

Aber um Einfaches geht es auch gar nicht, wenn es in der Kunst um Handwerk geht. Ein solcher Eindruck kann nur entstehen, wenn man vergisst, wie schwierig handgefertigte Dinge und wie schlicht dagegen oft die Kopfgeburten sind, die man eindeutig, restlos und erschöpfend in Sprache übersetzen kann. Eine Kunst hingegen, die im Anfassen und Durcharbeiten entsteht – sei es des Tons, des Linoleums, des Holzes oder der Farbsubstanzen – um aus den Materialien ein Ergebnis herauszukitzeln, das mehr ist als nur eine Materialschlacht oder eine Illustration, sondern ein eigenständiges Bild wird, ein Ereignis, eine solche Kunst hat viel mit einer praktischen Erfahrung zu tun, der man allenfalls mit einer *Theorie der Praxis* beikommen kann, wie Pierre Bourdieu sie benannt hat.

In seinem neuen Buch *The Craftsman* (2008, deutsch *Handwerk*, 2009) hat Richard Sennett kürzlich eine solche neue Theorie der Praxis unternommen, in der es auch um die künstlerische Bedeutung des Handwerks geht, was letztlich auf eine Rehabilitierung hinausläuft. Denn die Vorherrschaft der ästhetischen Theorie über die Handarbeit ist das eigentlich Akademische in der Kunst in all seiner historischen und problematischen Bedeutung.

Coda / Als ich Norbert Prangenbergs neue Ölbilder zum ersten Mal gesehen habe, 2008 während des Aufbaus einer Ausstellung bei Karsten Greve in Köln, habe ich anschließend in mein Notizbuch geschrieben: „Die Aushändigung von Farbe". Schon Wochen später wusste ich nicht mehr ganz genau, was ich damit gemeint haben mochte, bin mir aber immer noch sicher, dass es in der Arbeit von Prangenberg vor allem darum geht – um die Aushändigung von Farbe.

Walter Grasskamp

in other words, to create an autonomous image or event – this kind of art has a lot to do with a form of practical experience that requires the application of a *theory of practice,* as defined by Pierre Bourdieu.

Richard Sennett recently outlined such a new theory of practice in his book *The Craftsman* (2008), which also focuses on the artistic importance of craftsmanship. This ultimately amounts to a rehabilitation of craft, as the dominance of aesthetic theory over craft is the truly academic dimension within art, in all its historical and problematic significance.

Coda / After seeing Norbert Prangenberg's new oil paintings for the first time, during the installation of his 2008 exhibition at Galerie Karsten Greve in Cologne, I wrote in my notebook: "the handing out of colour". Only weeks later, I could no longer say what I had meant by that, but I am still sure that this is precisely what Prangenberg's work is about – the handing out of colour.

Walter Grasskamp
Translated by Jacqueline Todd

Robinson

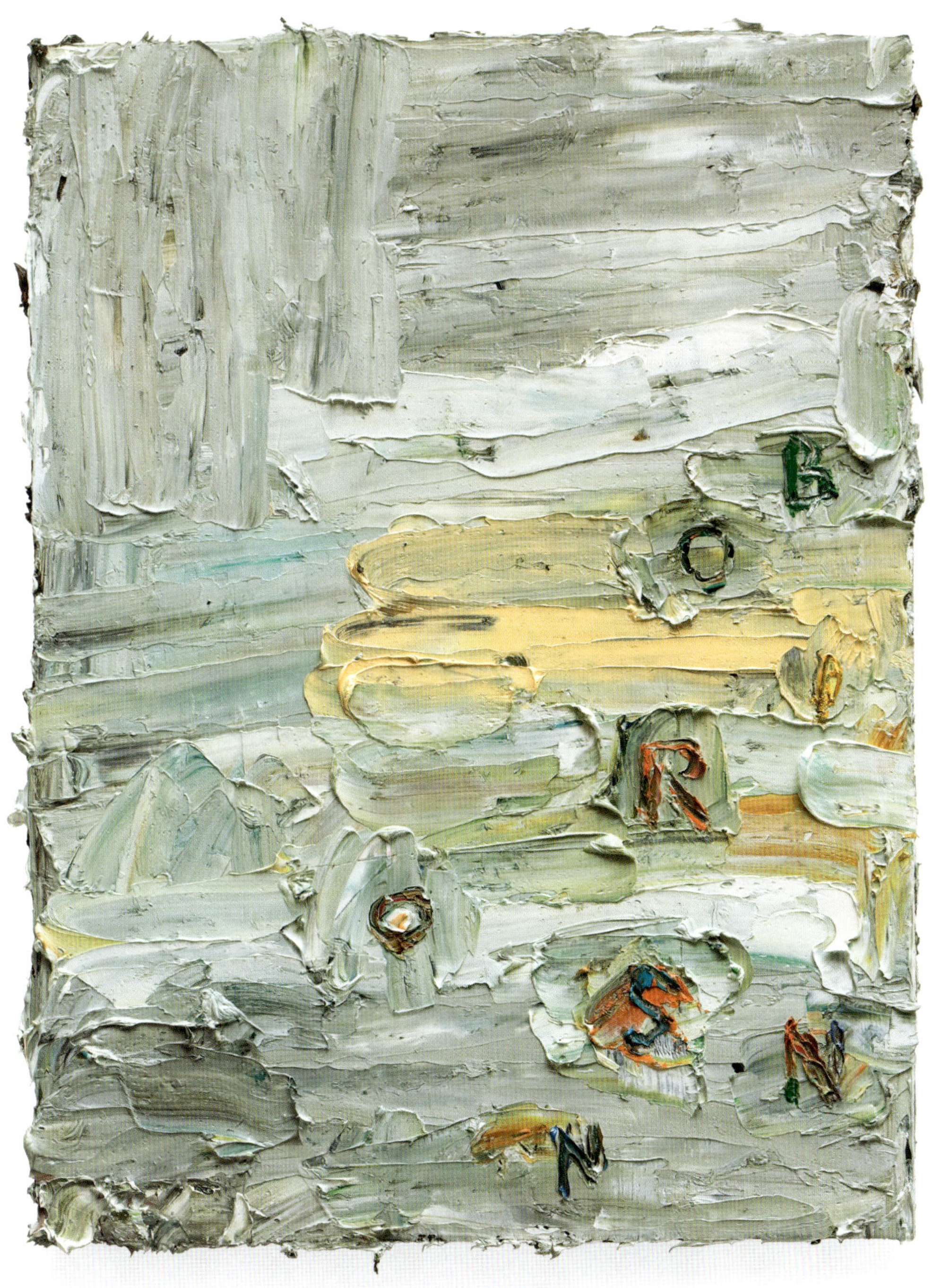

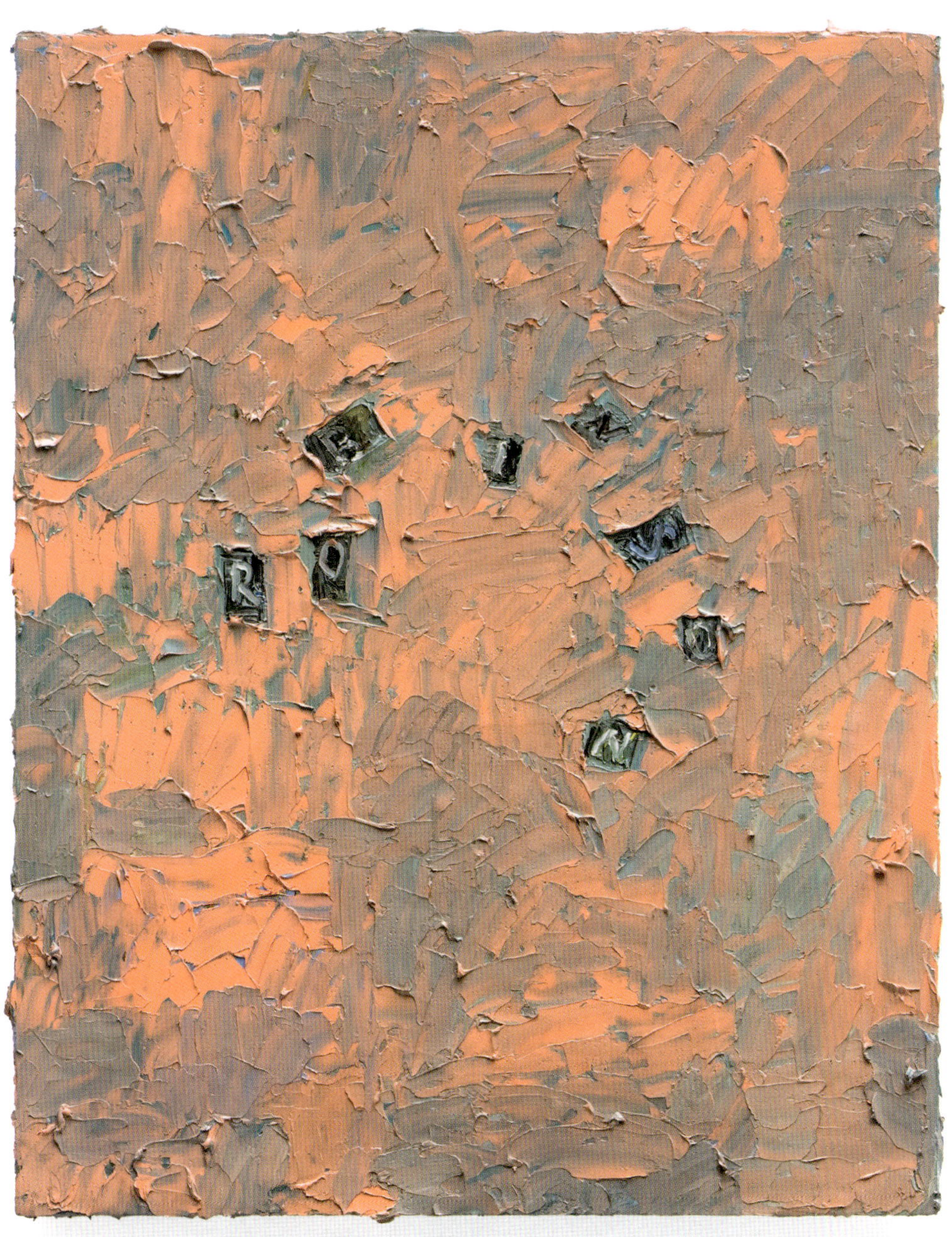

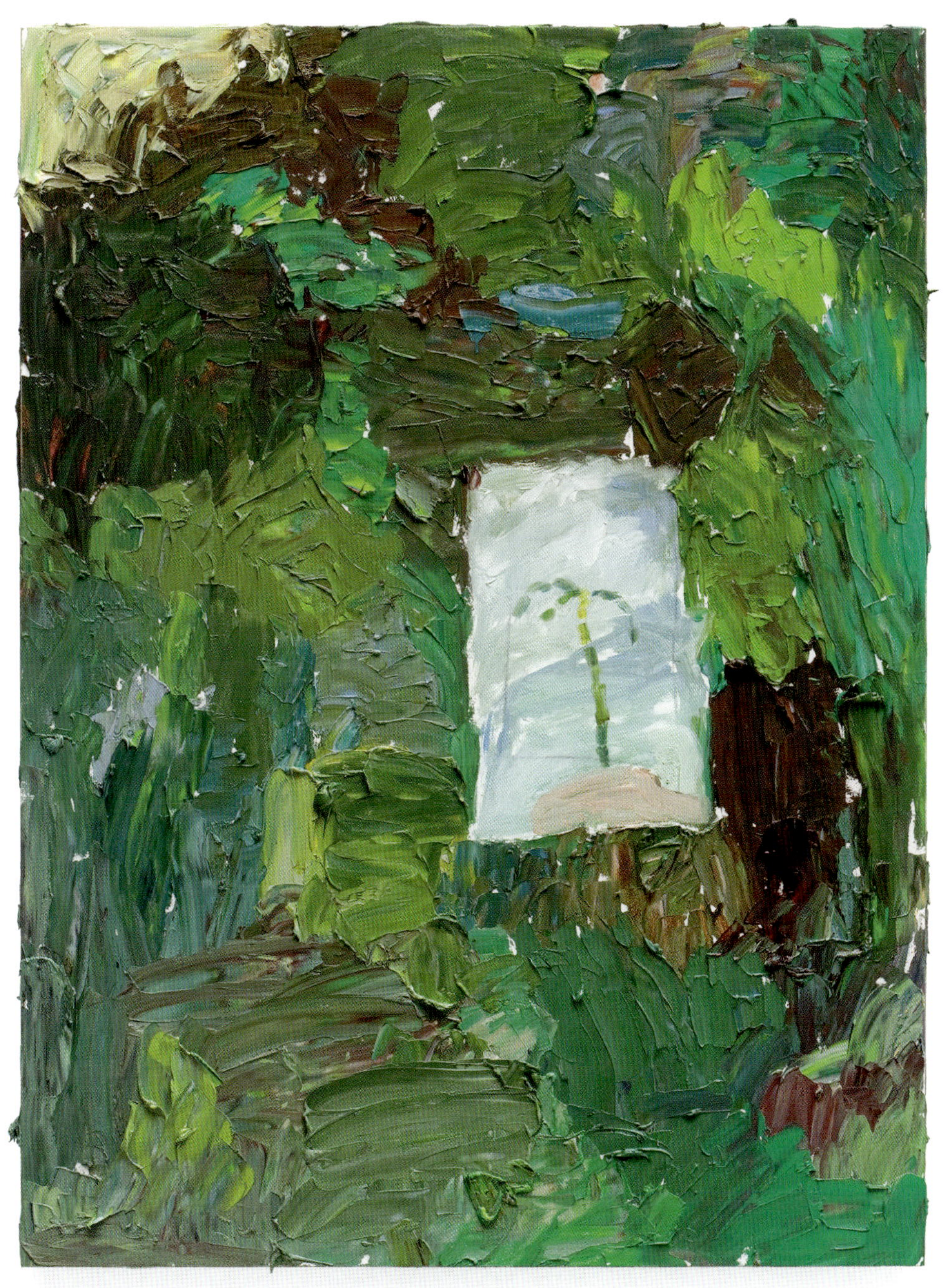

Bilder

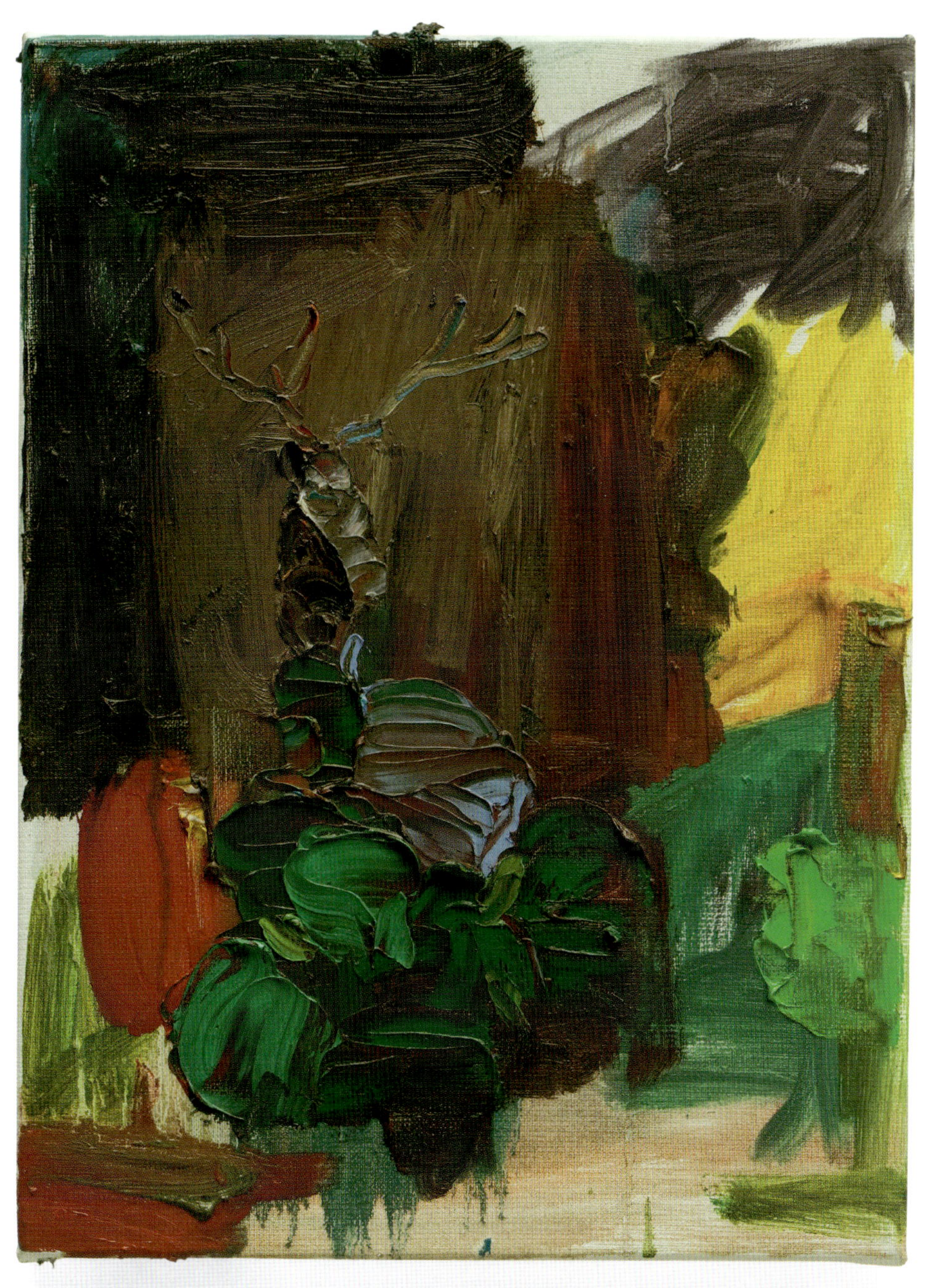

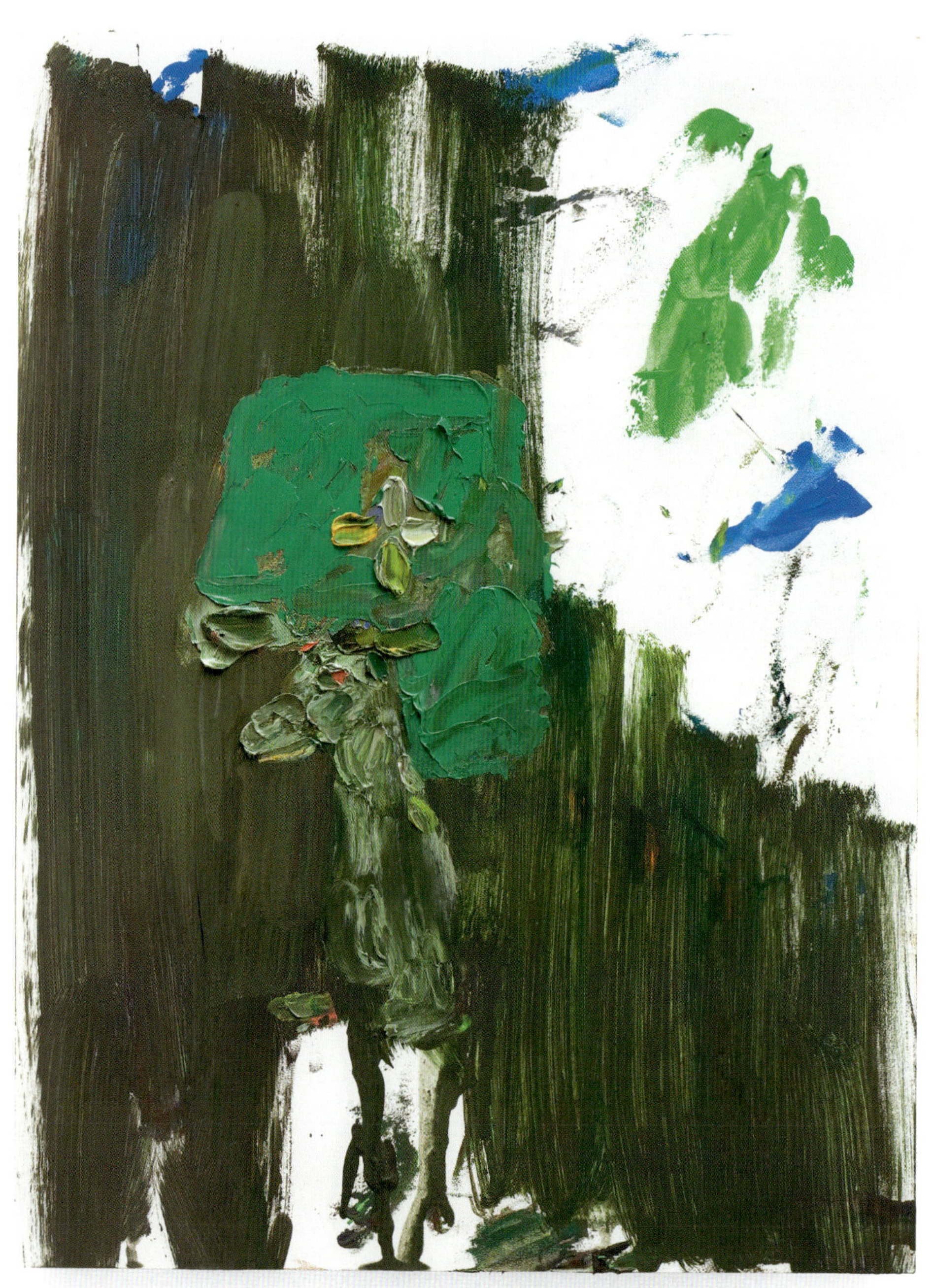

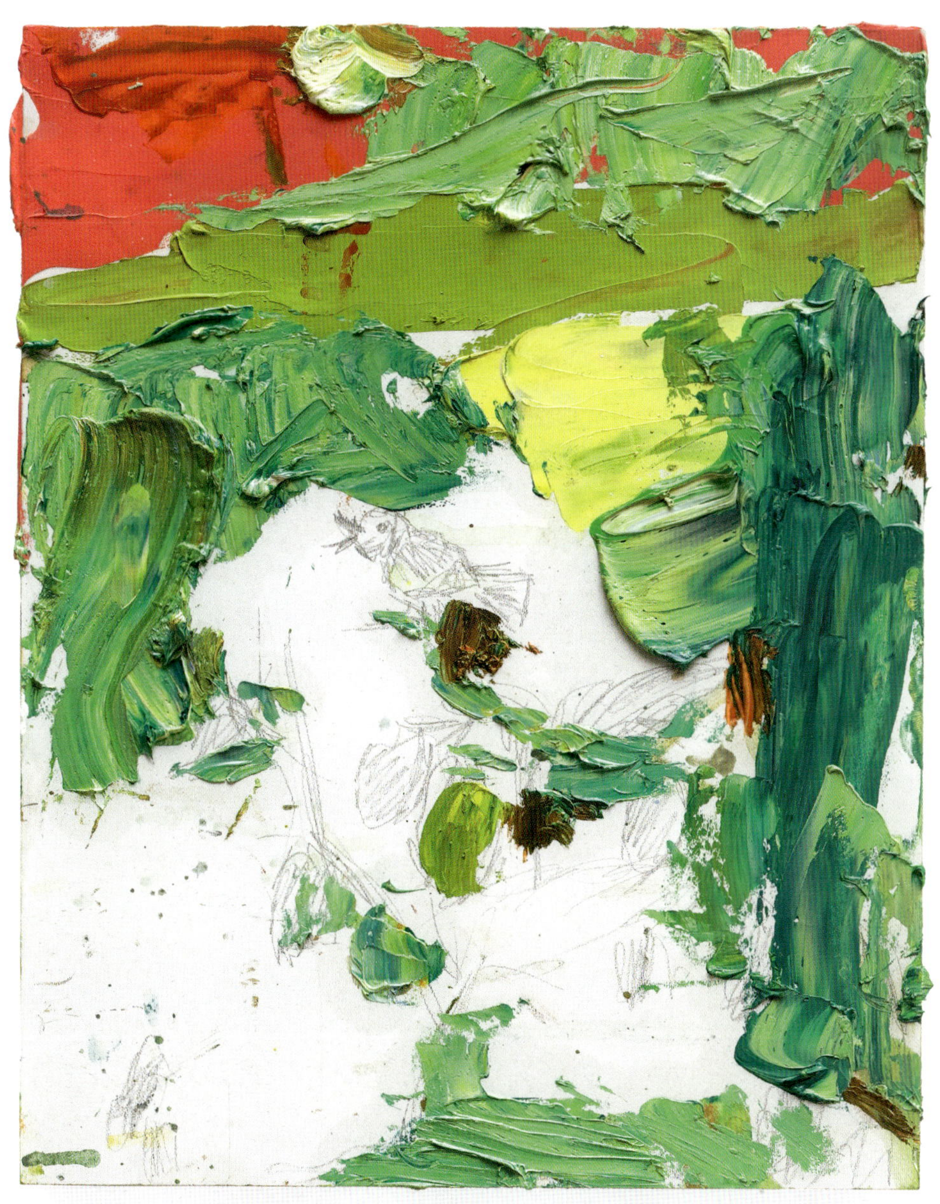

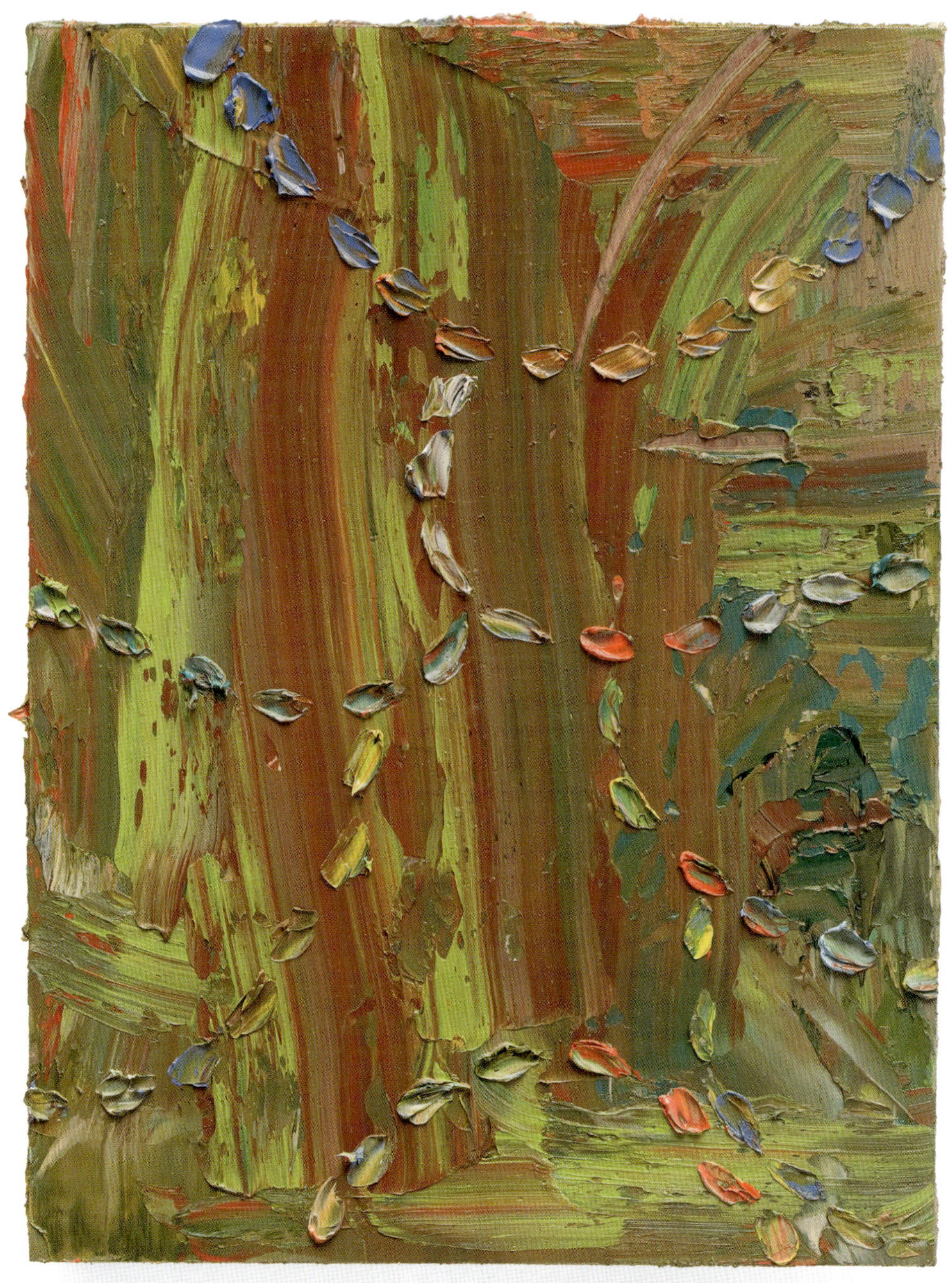

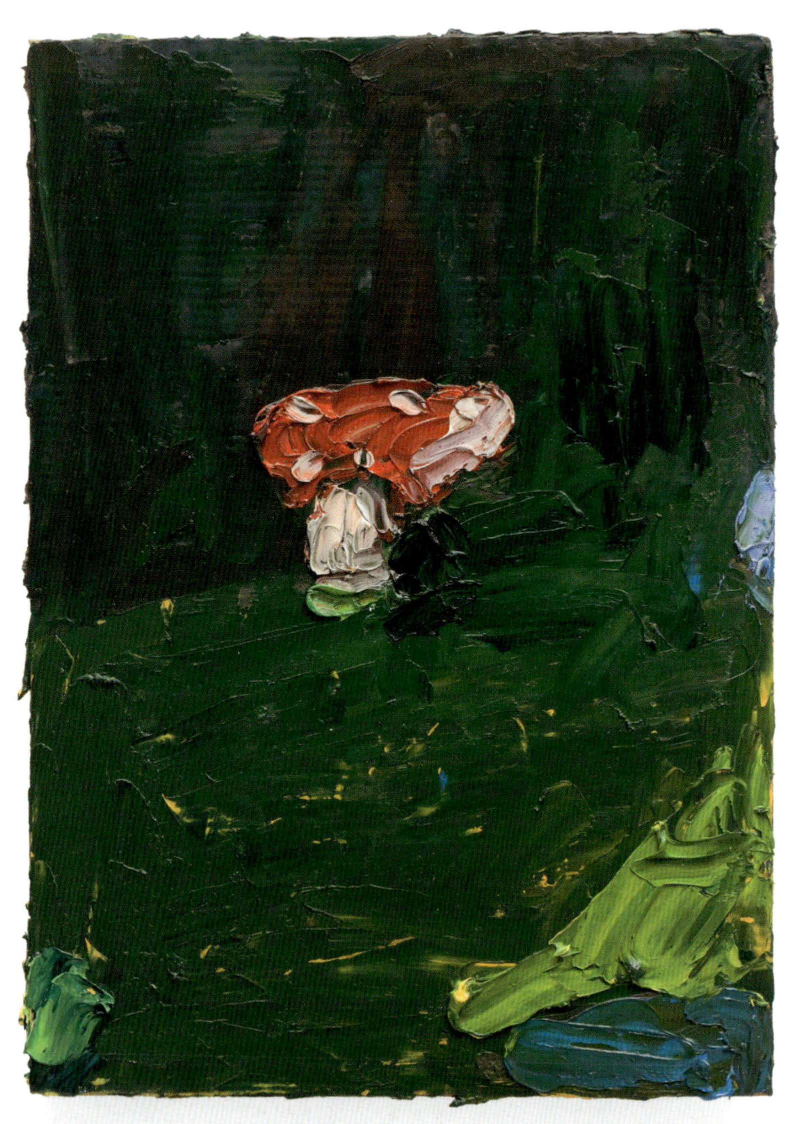

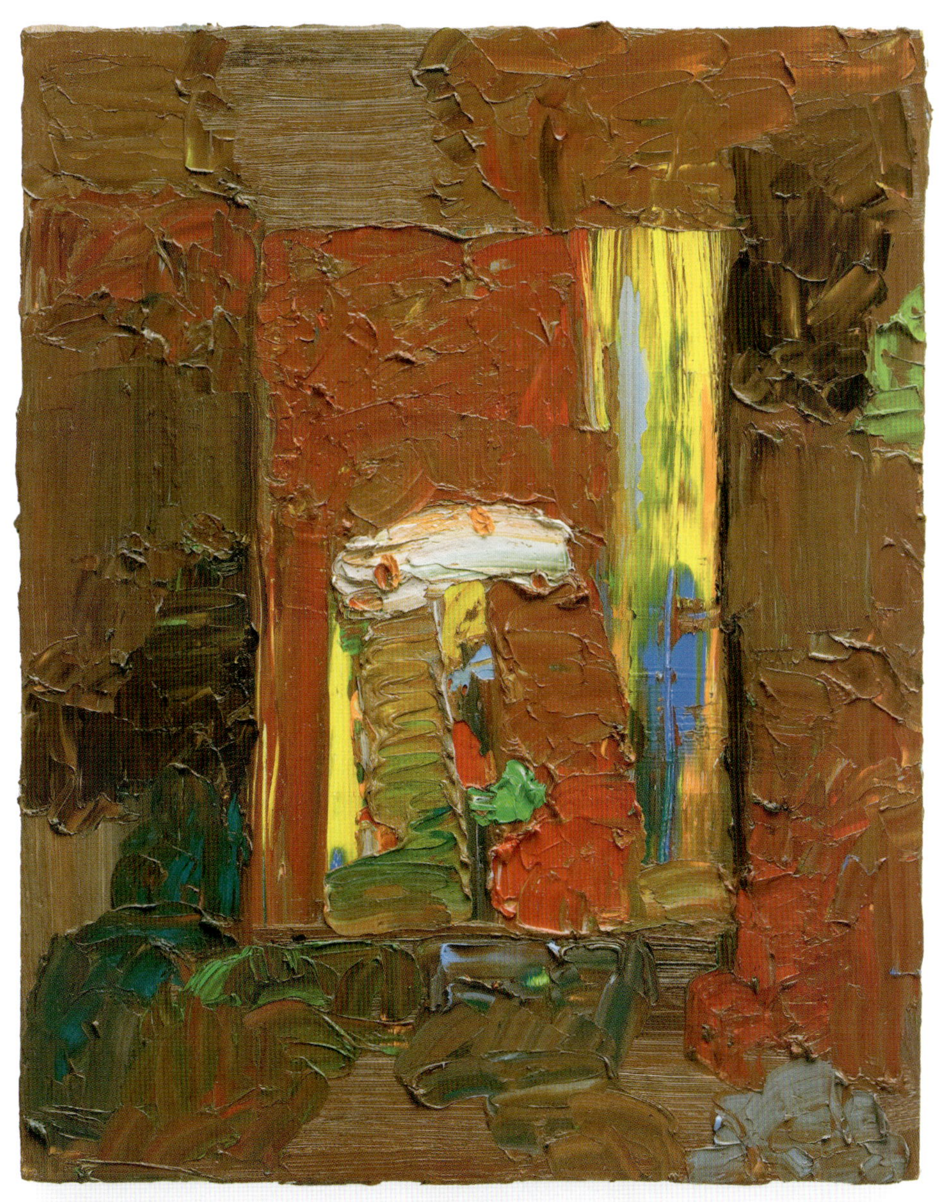

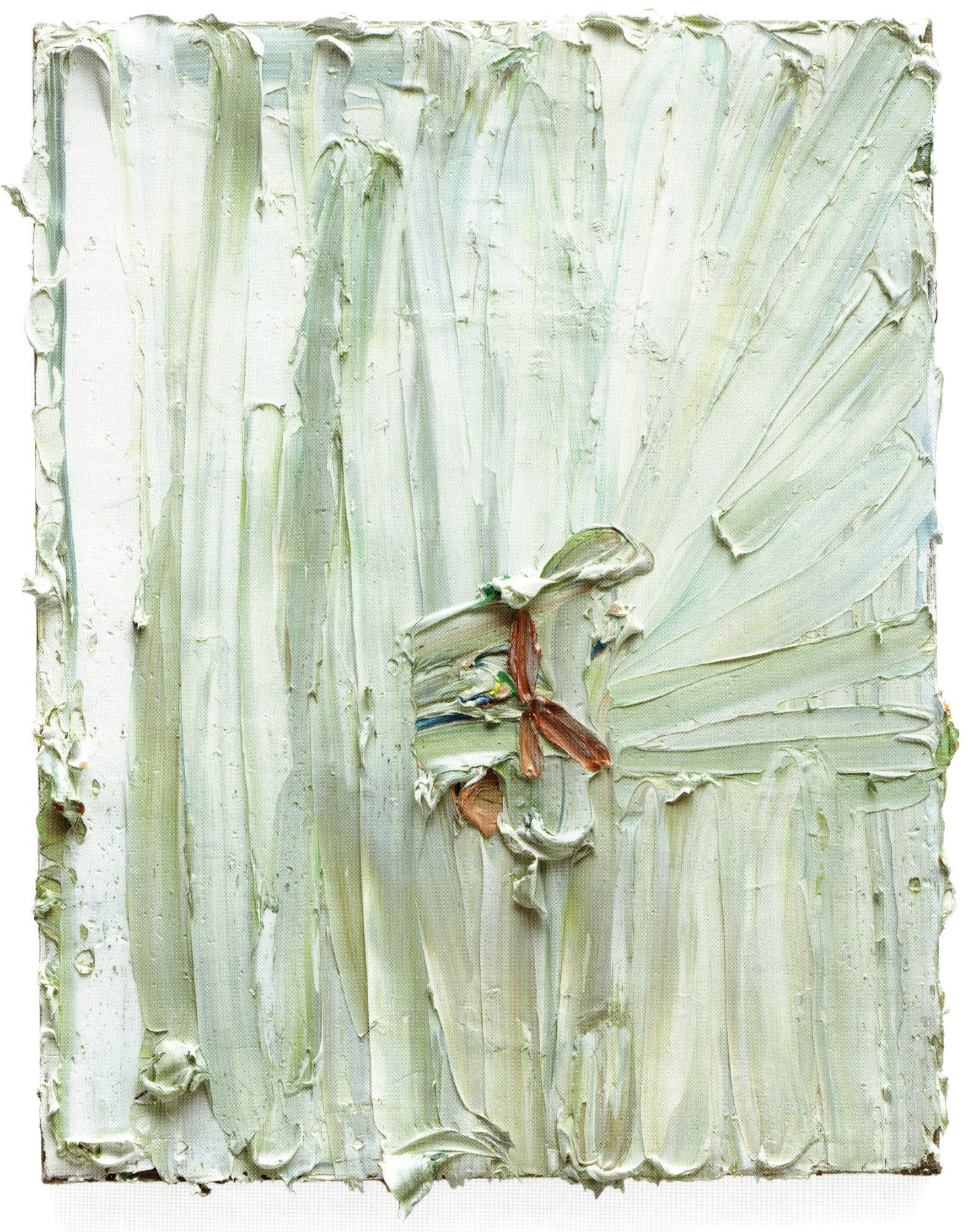

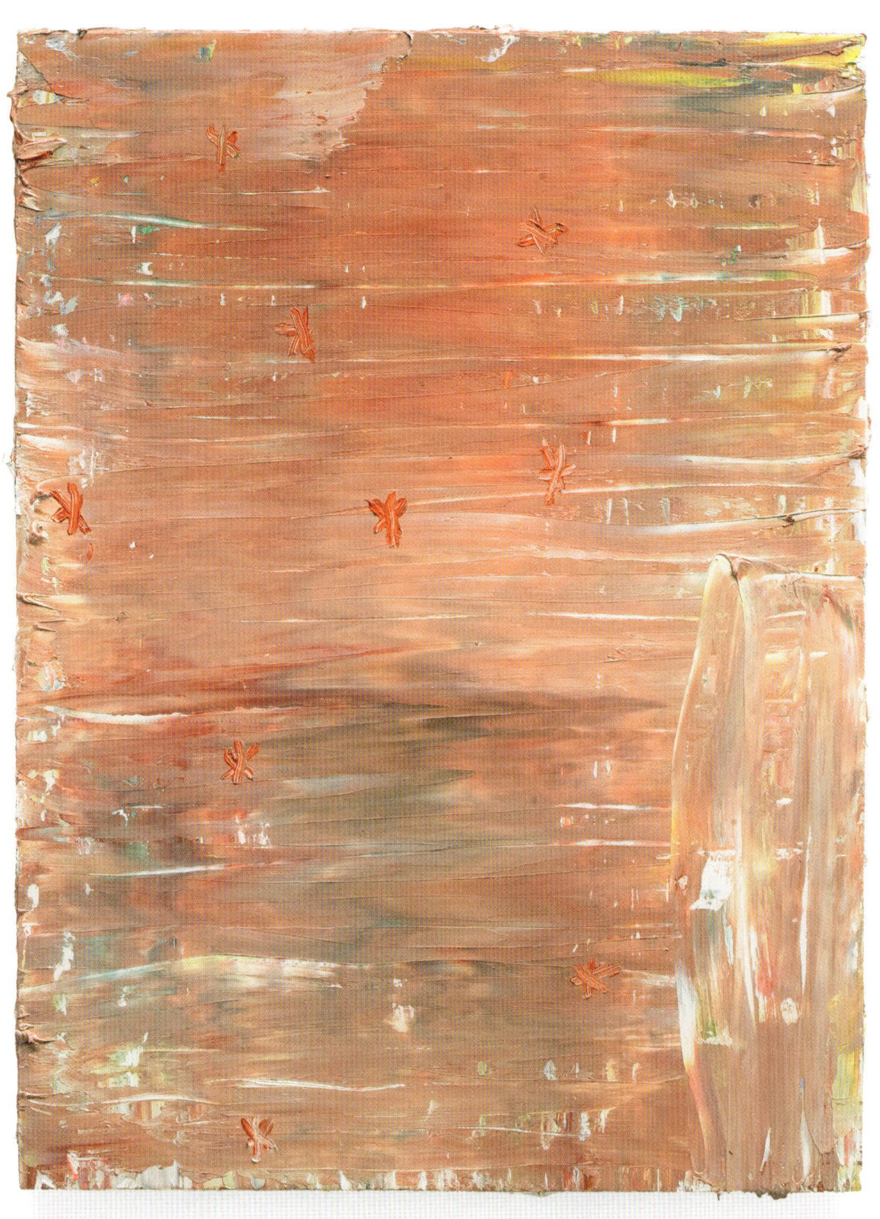

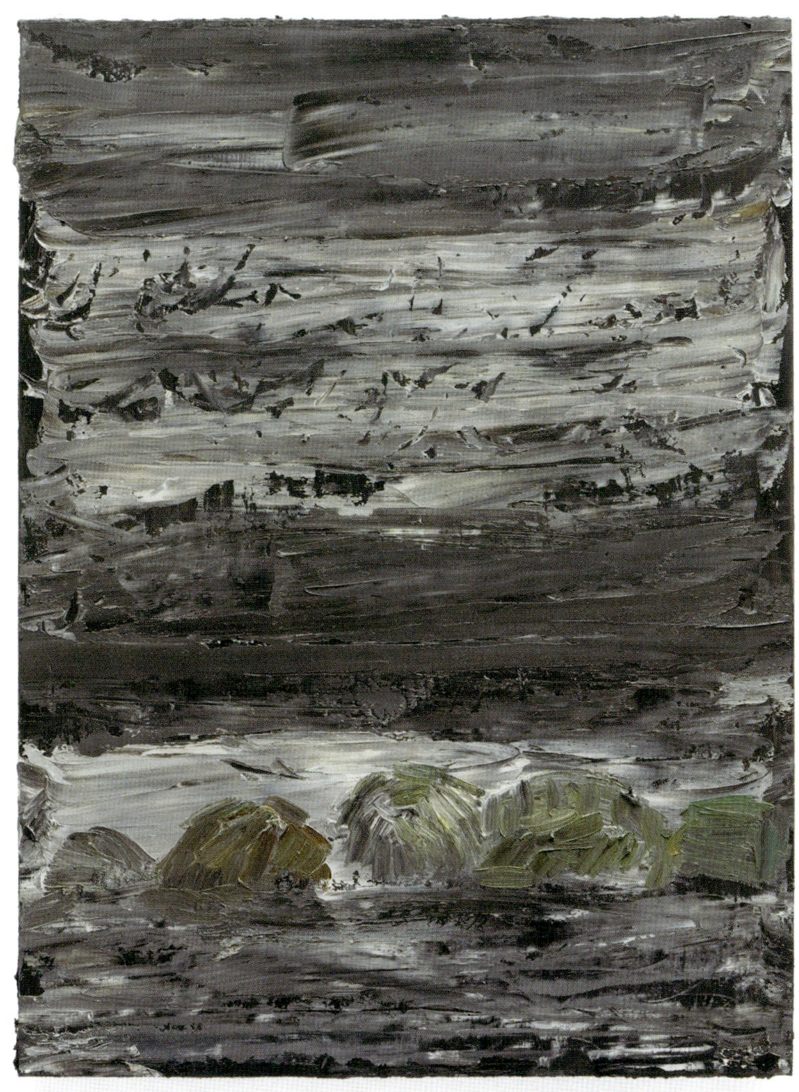

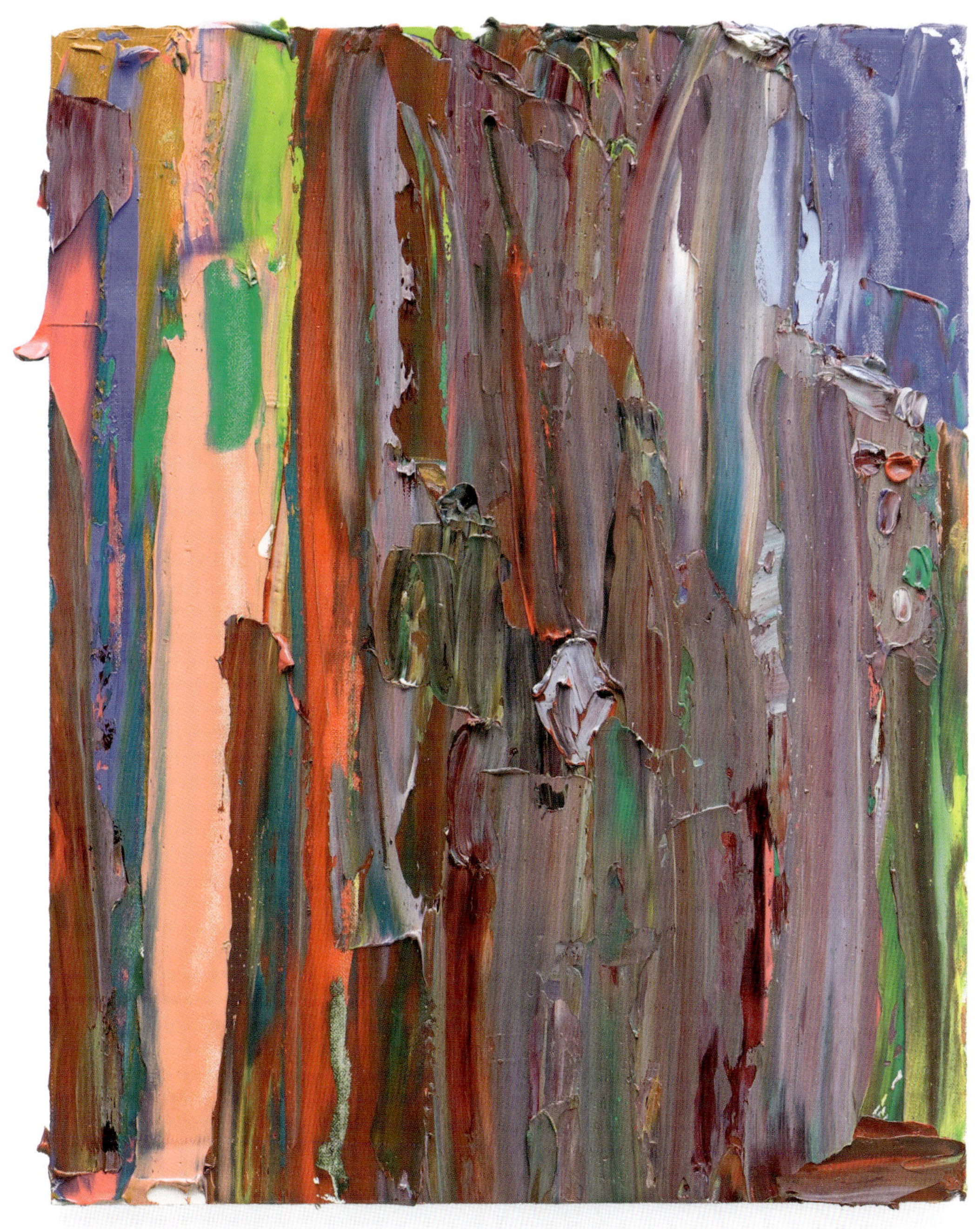

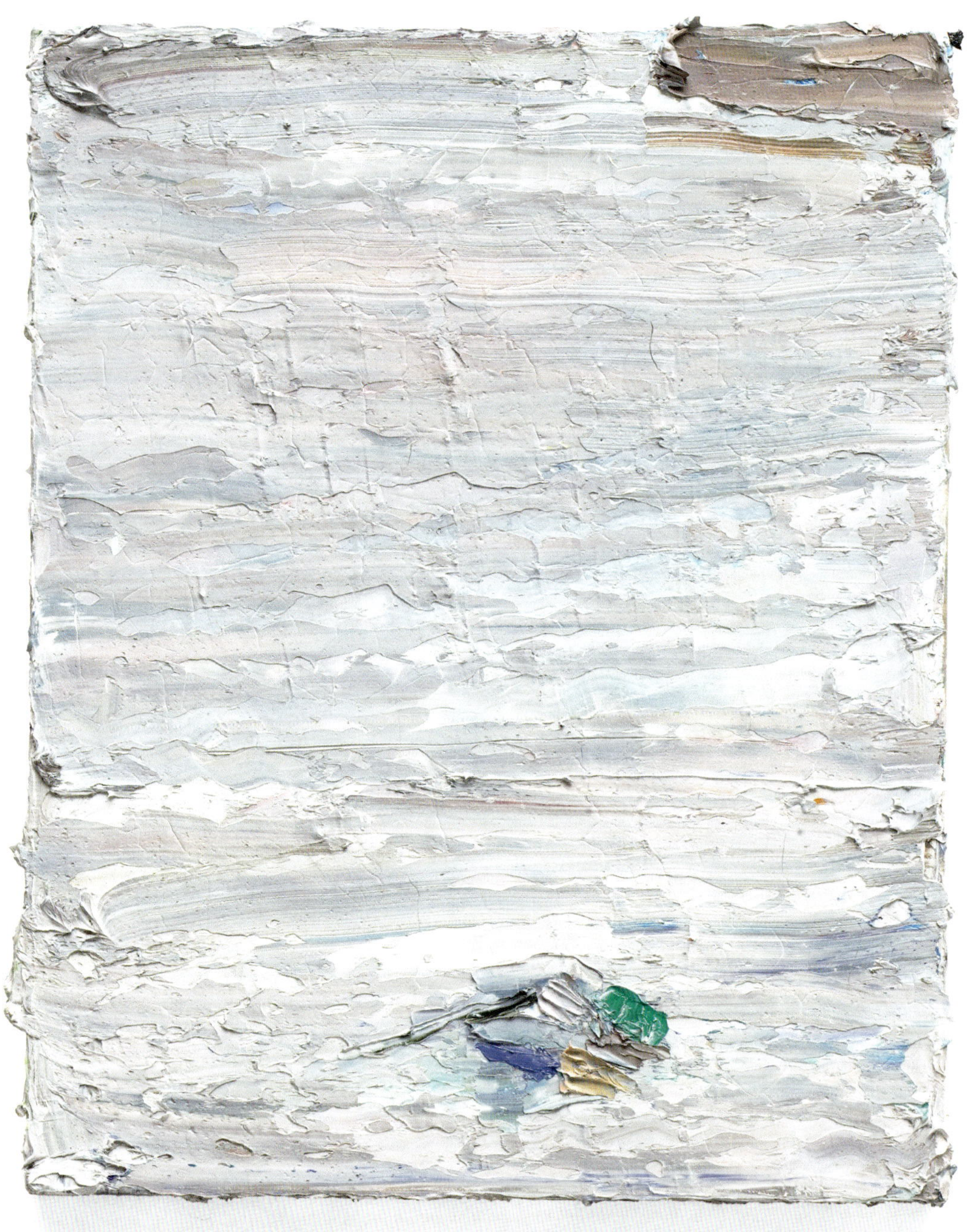

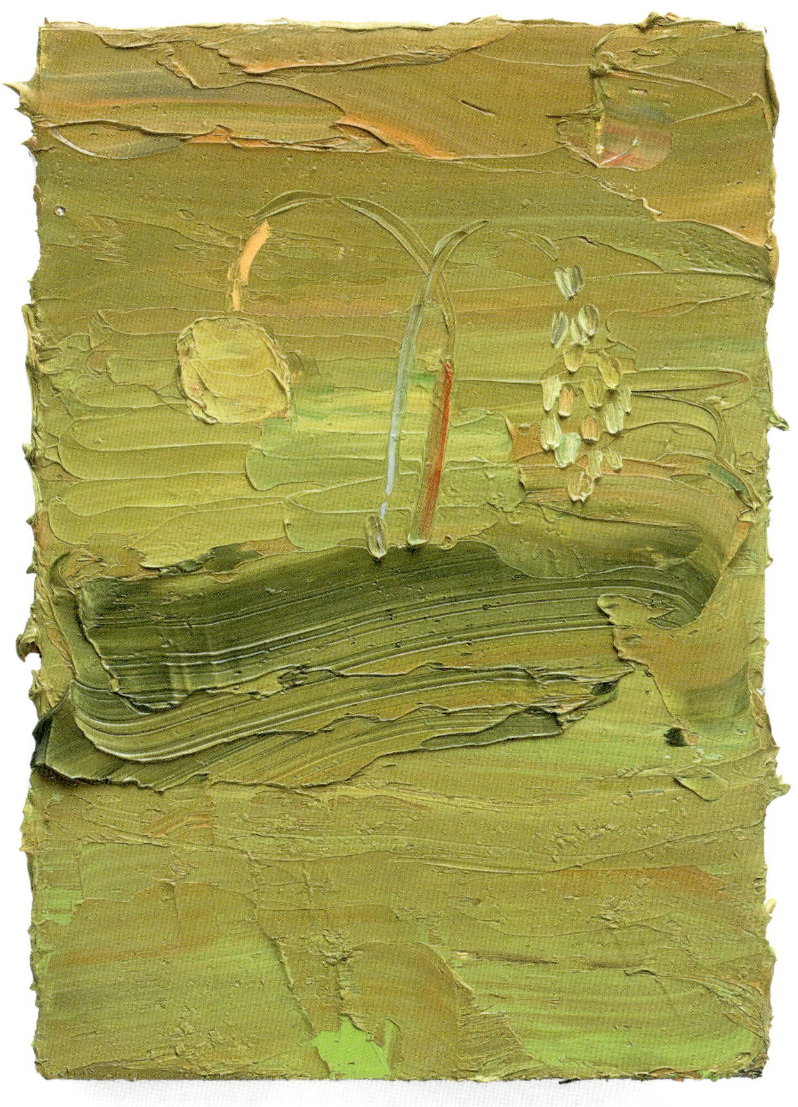

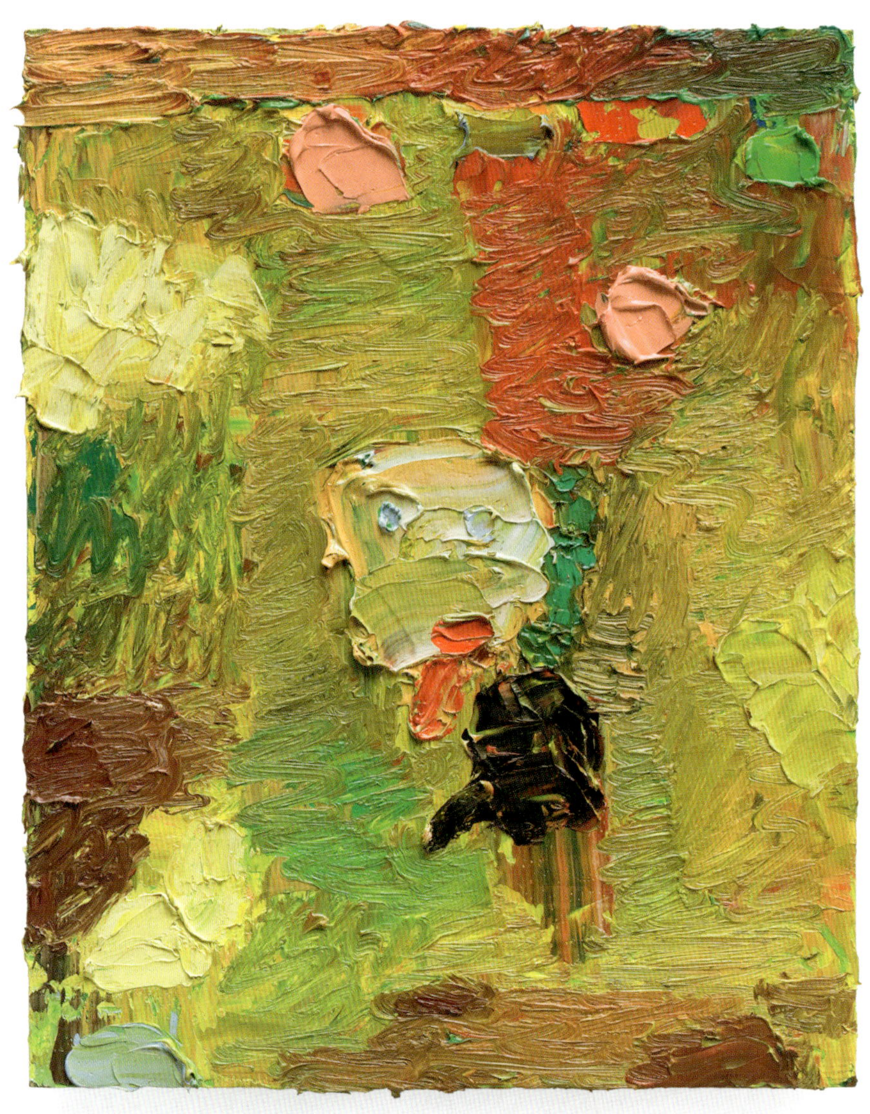

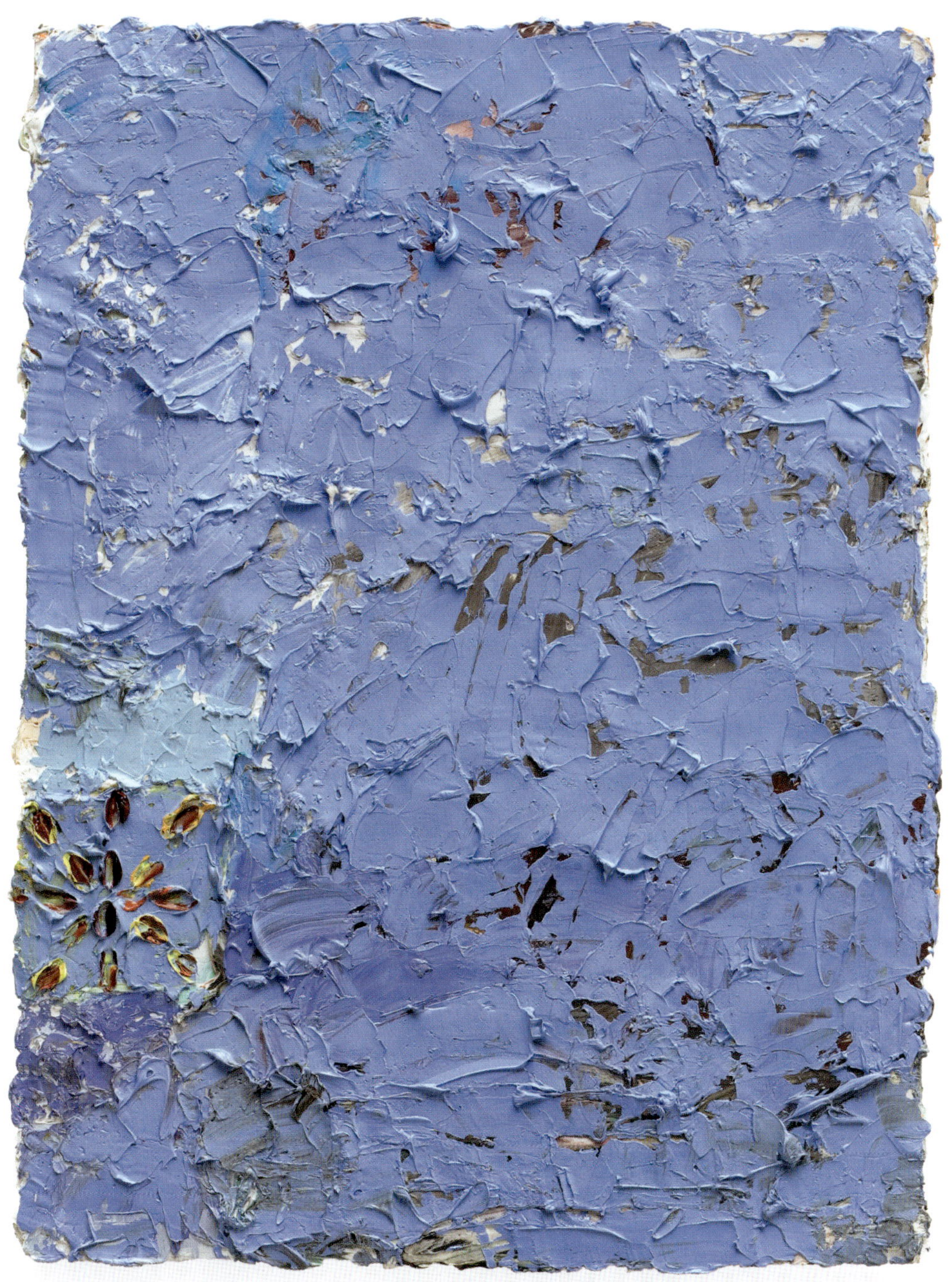

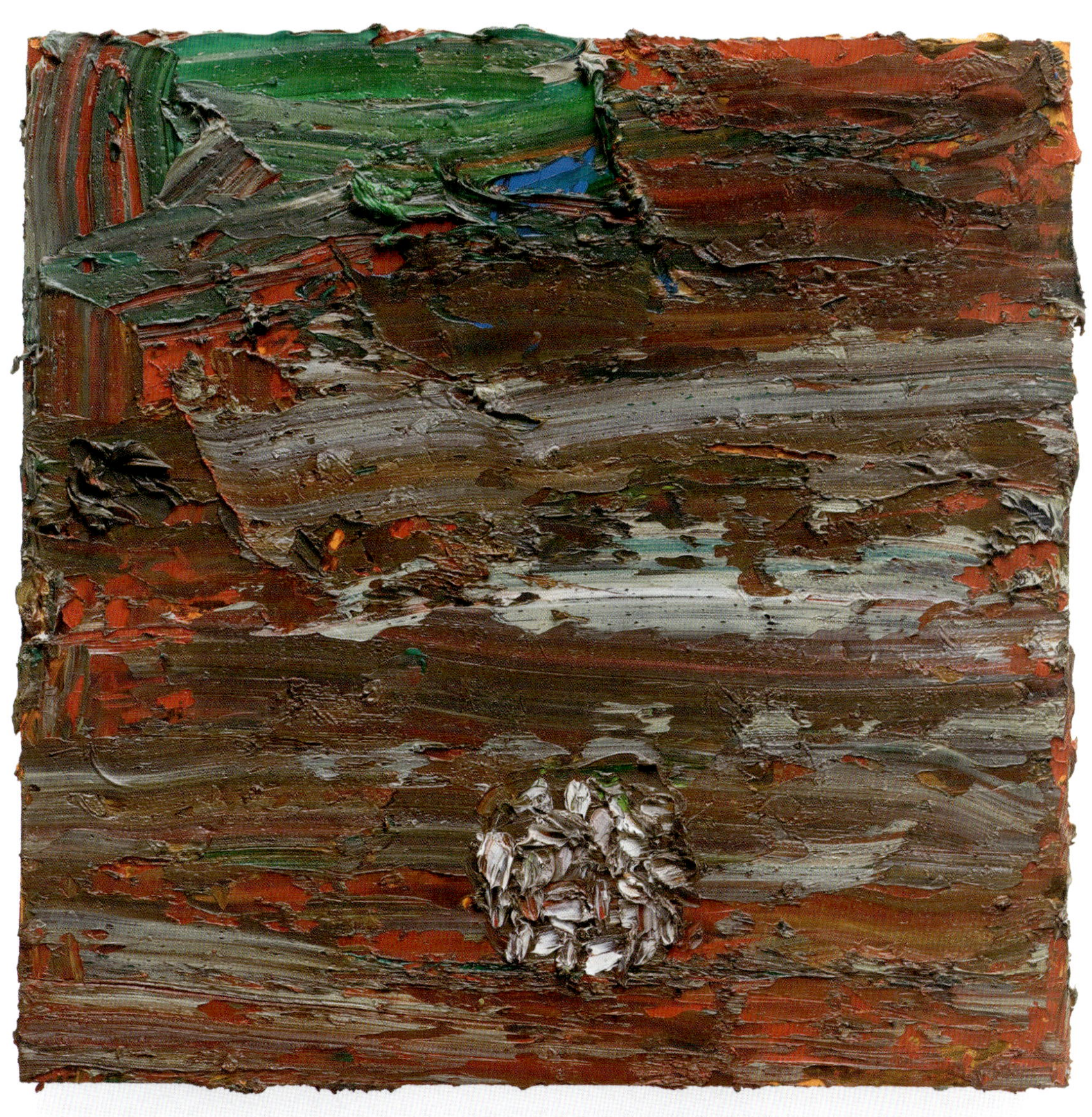

Abstrakt

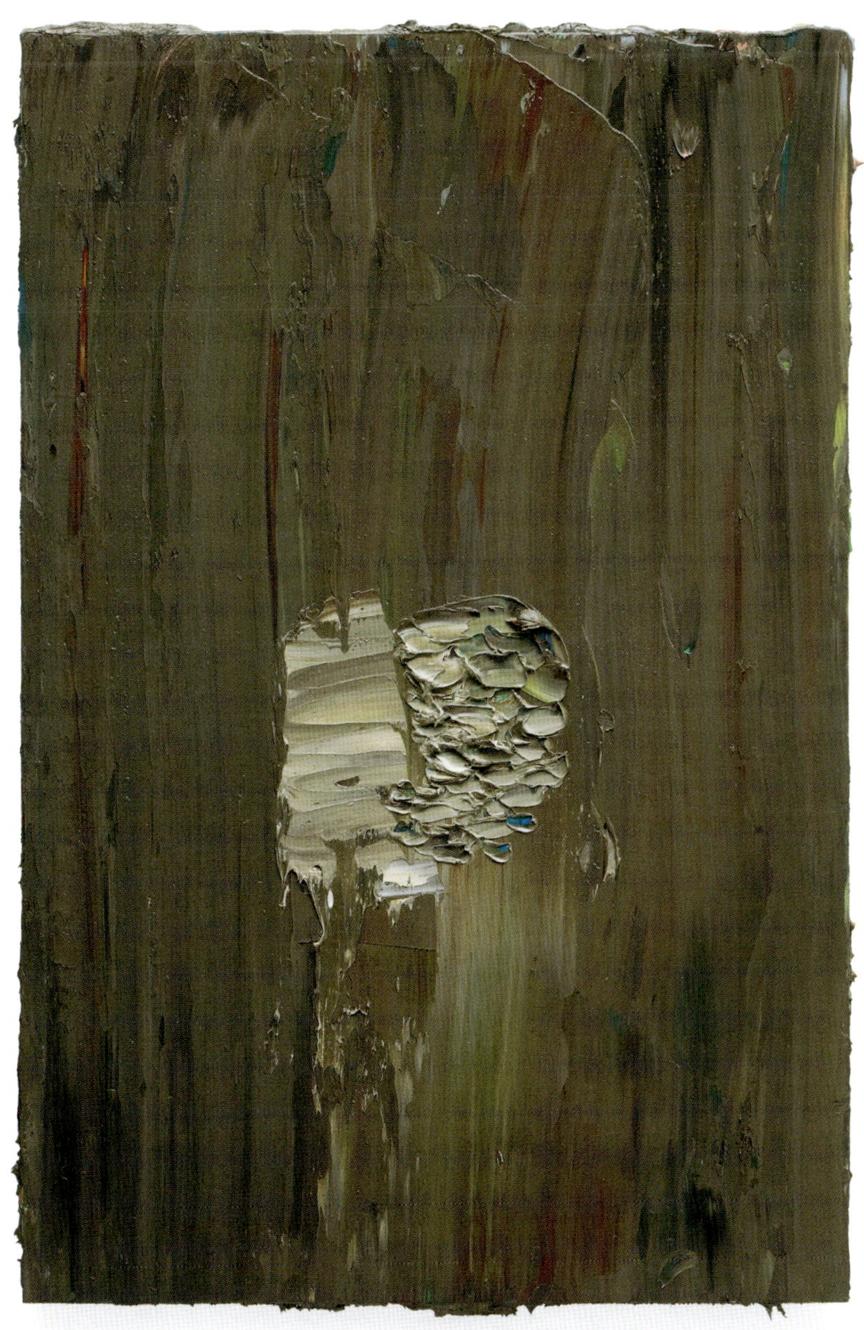

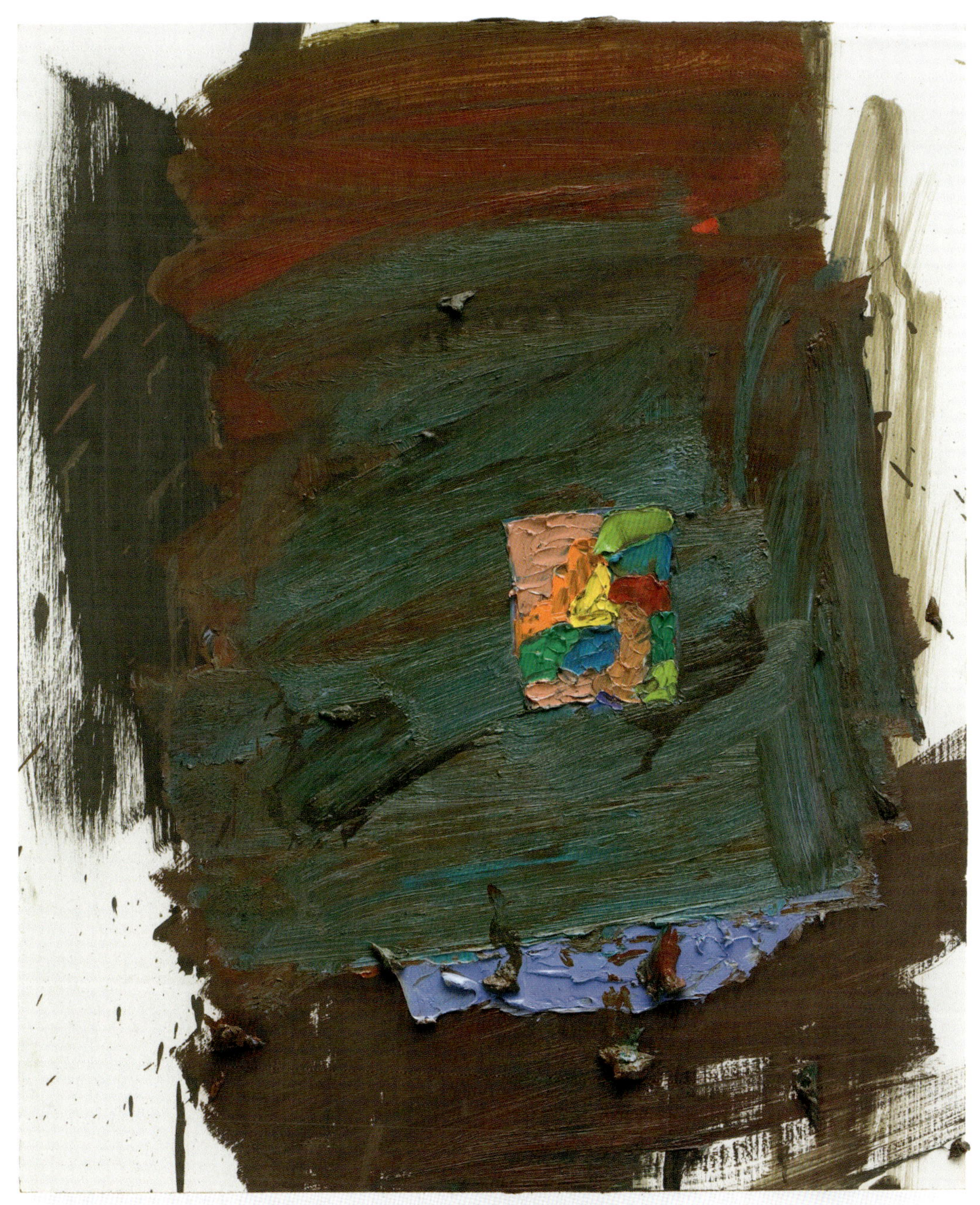

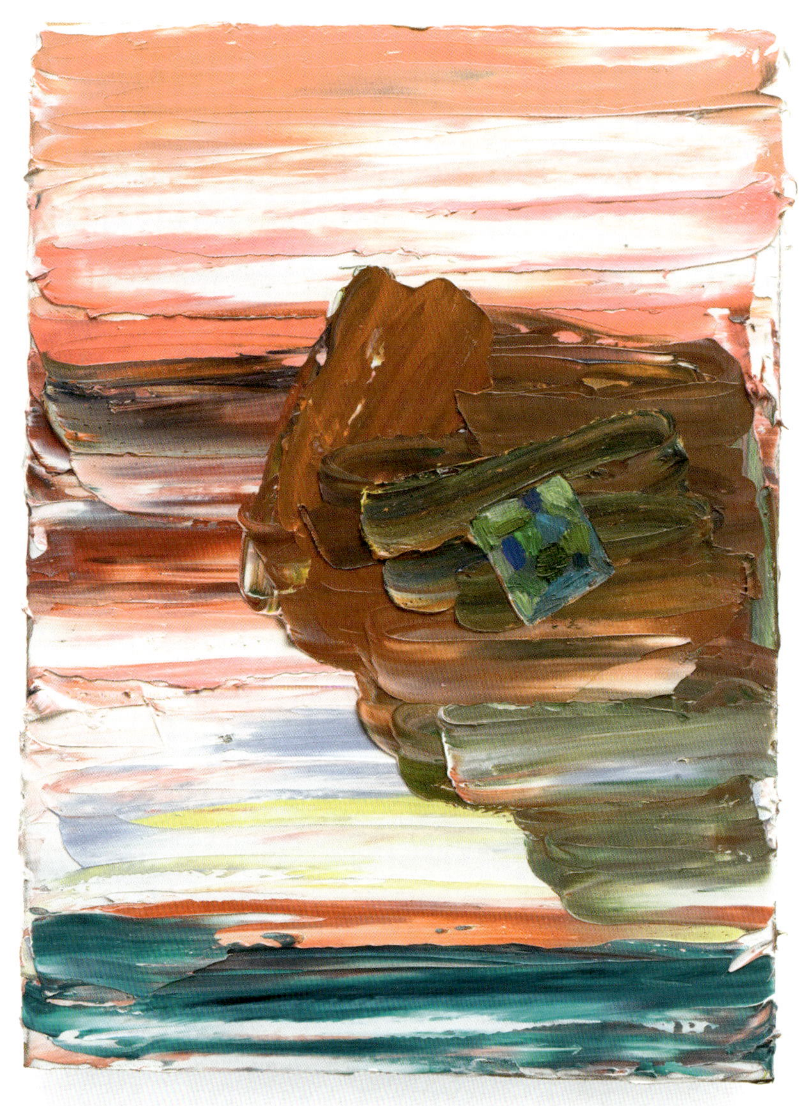

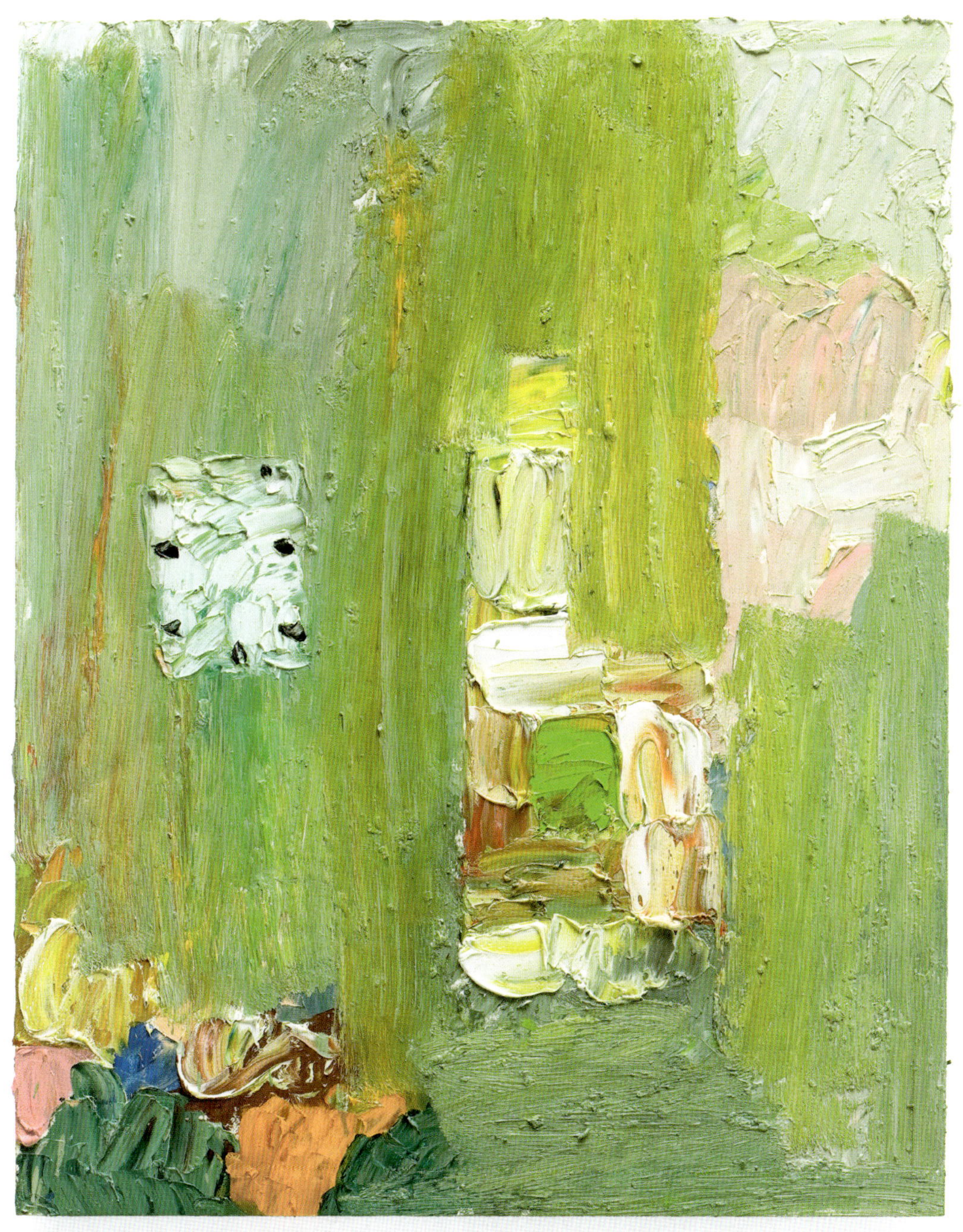

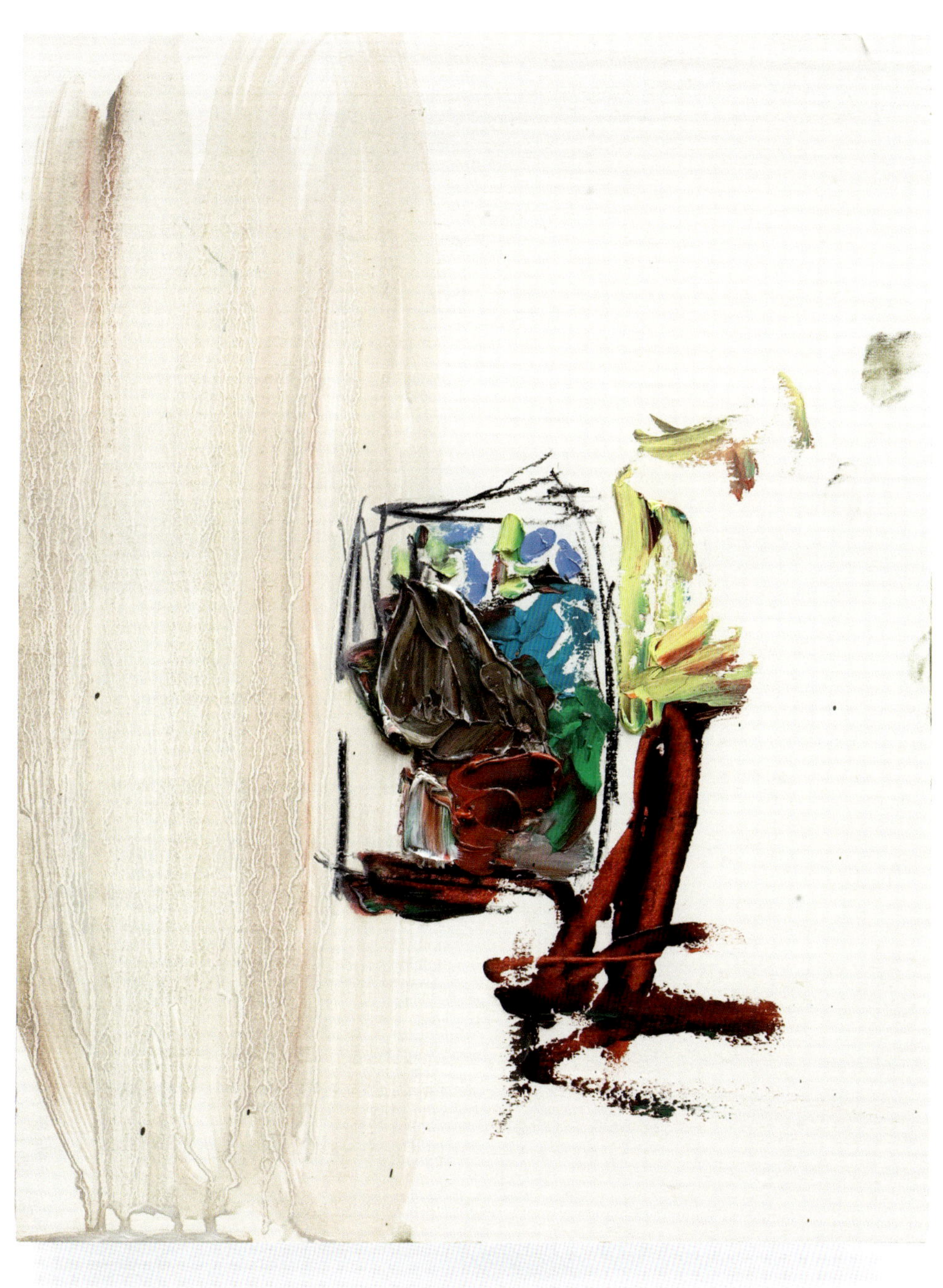

Tengus

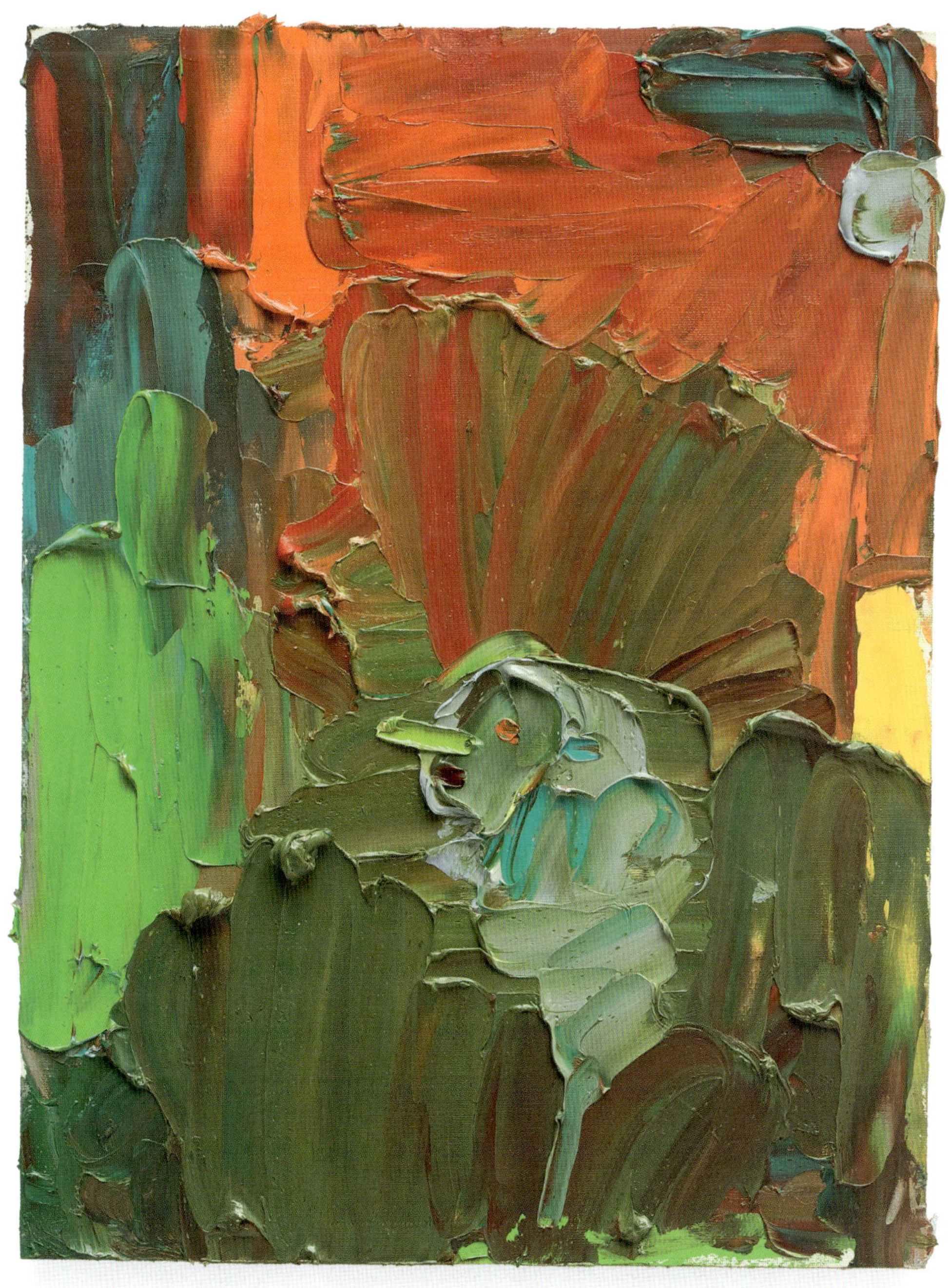

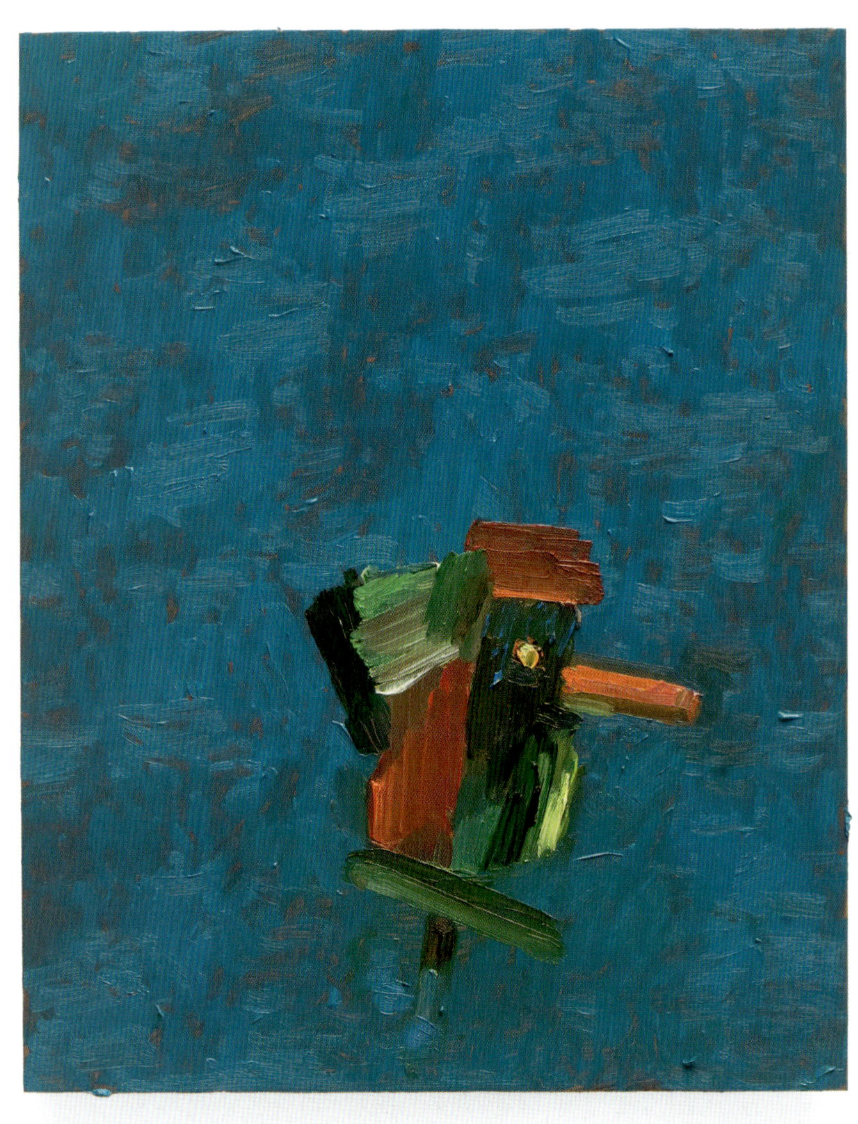

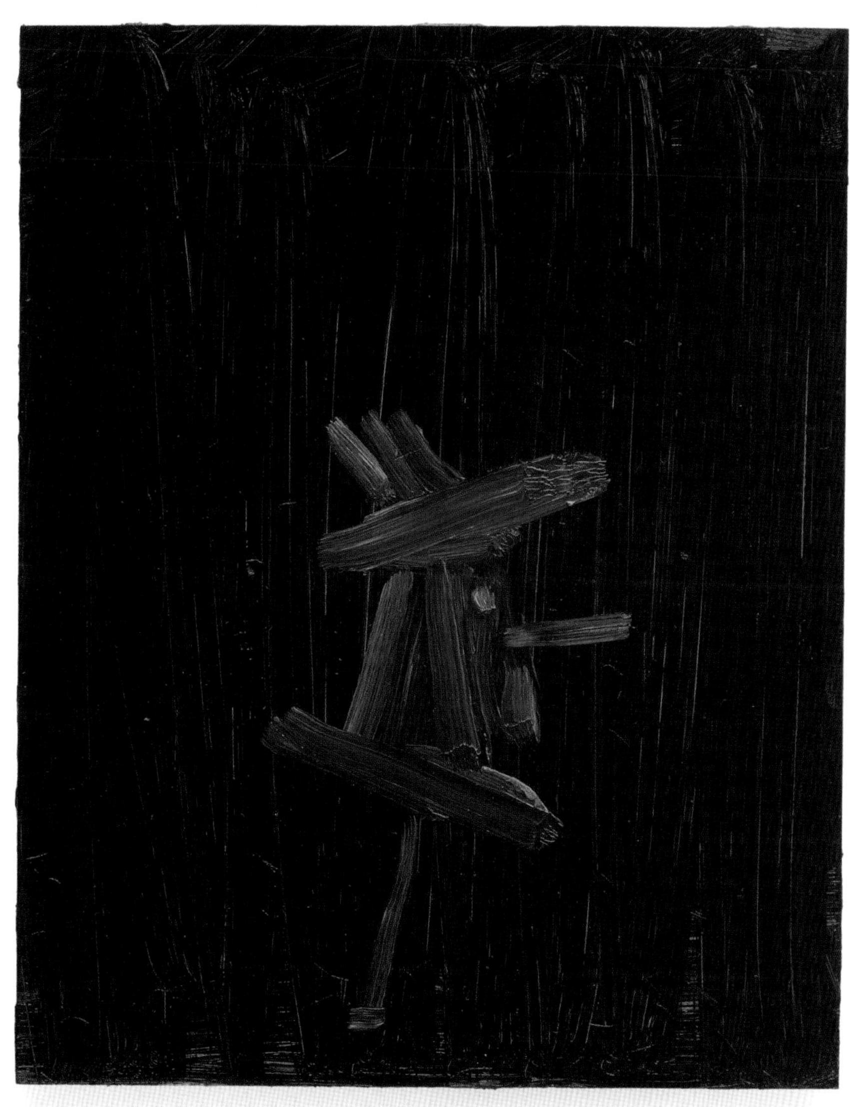

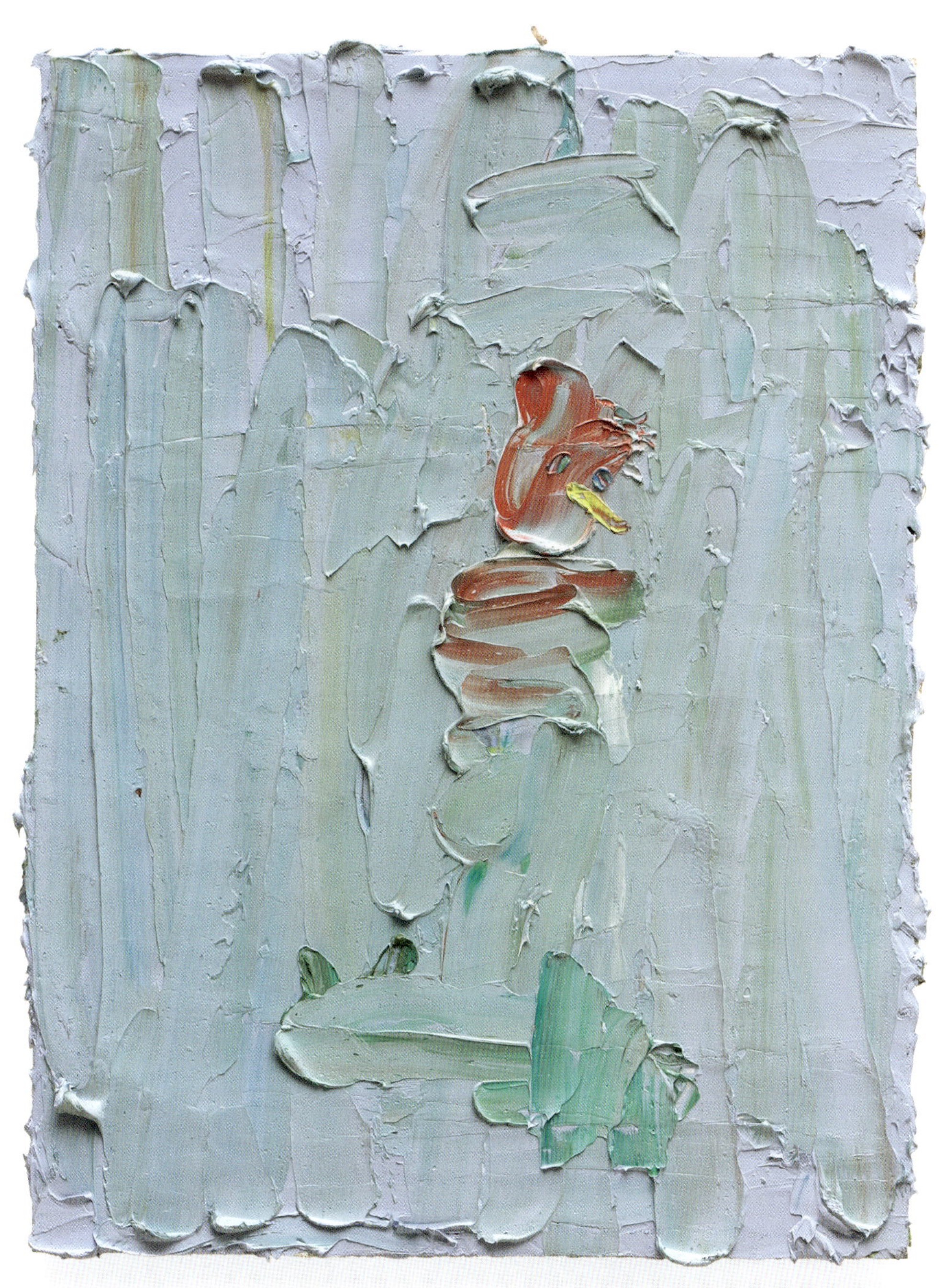

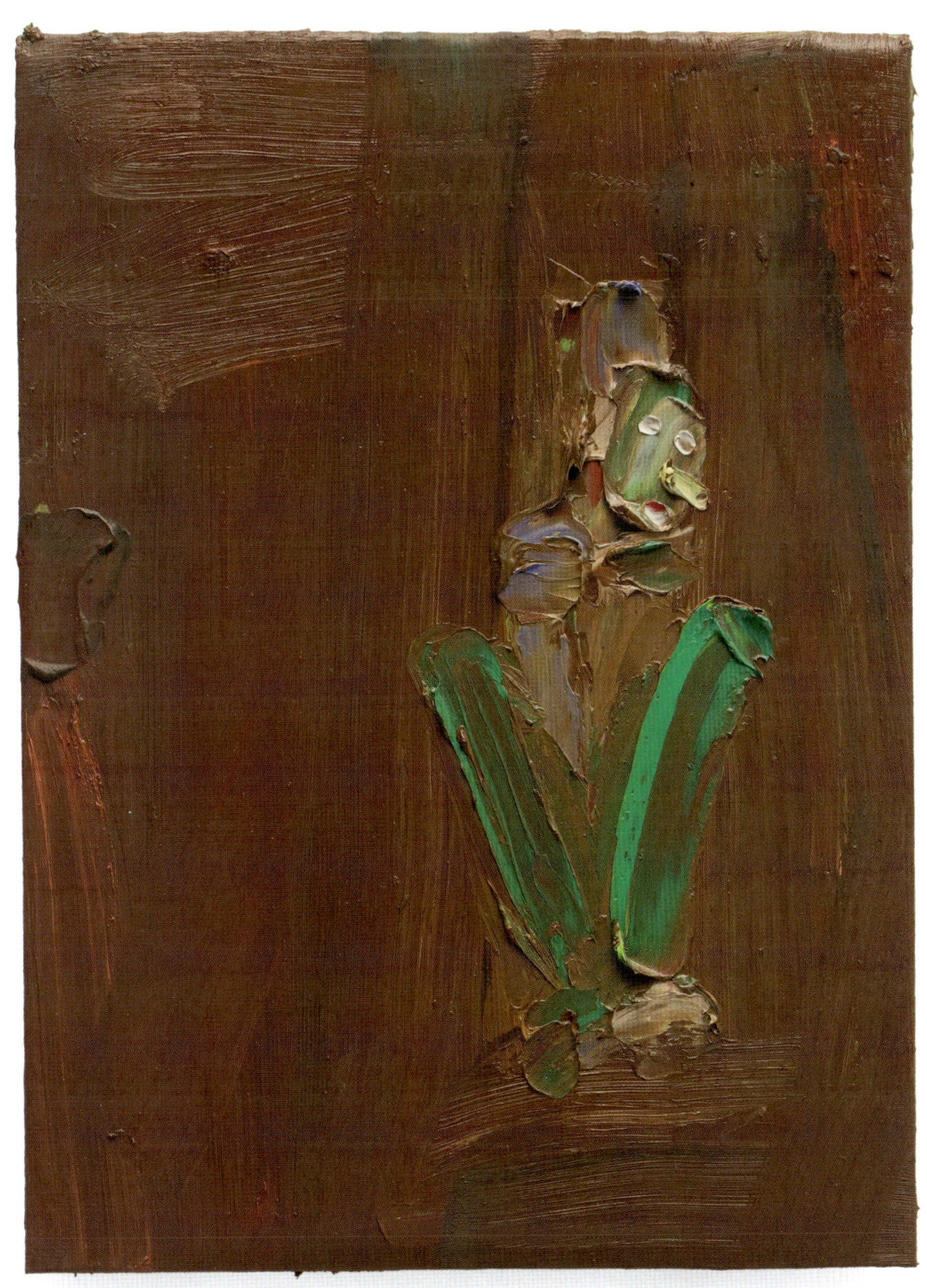

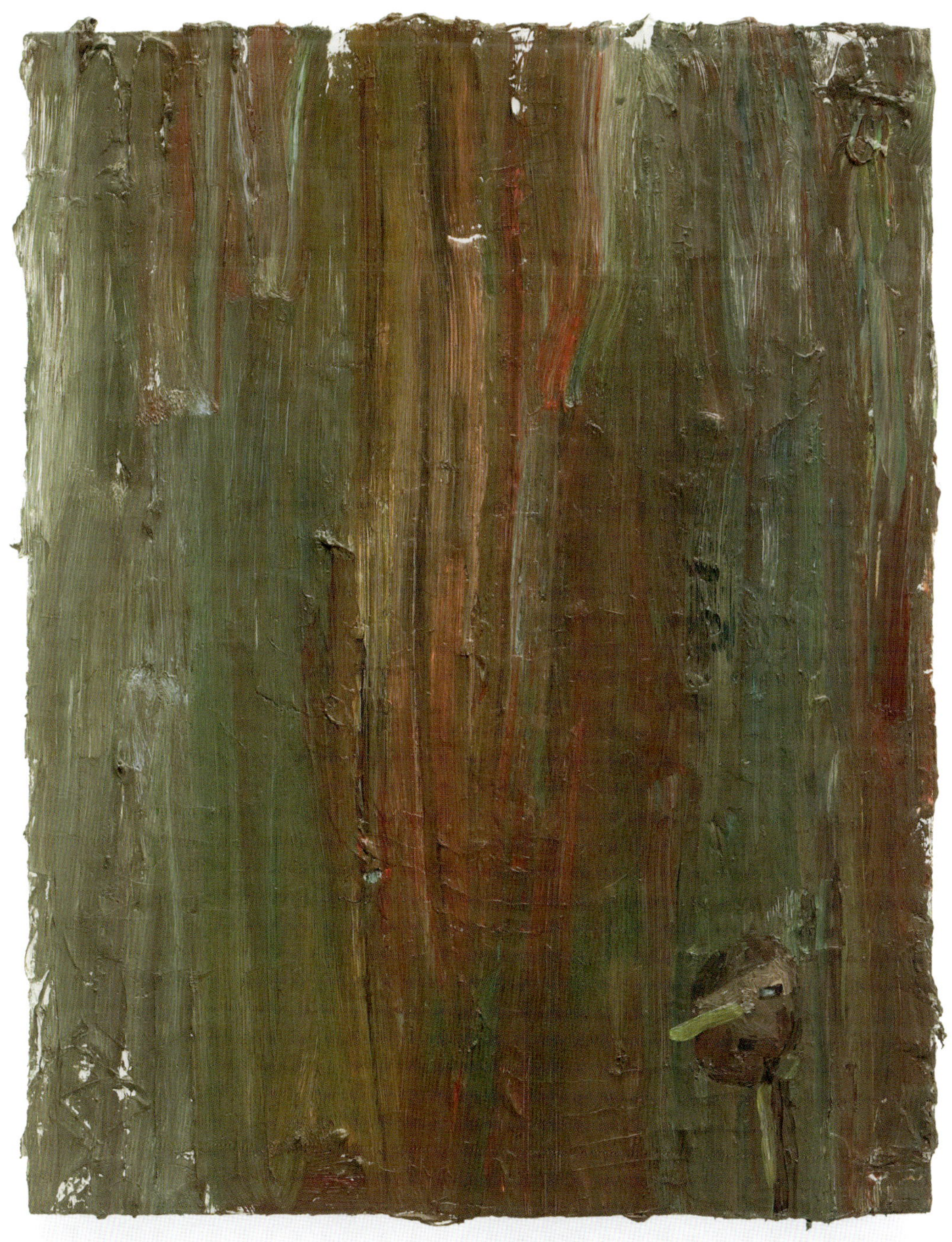

Abbildungen
Plates

5 Der Maler (30.10.), 2008
   Öl auf Holz, 42 × 29.5 cm

8 Zyklop (01.07.), 2009
   Öl auf Karton, 30 × 24 cm

9 Der Maler (29.10.), 2008,
   Öl auf Holz, 30 × 21 cm

11 Face (29.01.), 2008
   Öl auf Karton, 30 × 24 cm

12 Bild (05.10.), 2009
   Öl auf Holz, 45 × 35 cm

13 Kind (03.01.), 2009
   Öl auf Holz, 40 × 35 cm

15 für Constantin (26.08.)
   2009, Öl auf Holz, 40 × 30 cm

17 Pinocchio (10.02.), 2009
   Öl auf Pappe, 30 × 24 cm

18 Face (08.02.), 2009
   Öl auf Holz, 30 × 24 cm

19 Face (12.12.), 2008
   Öl auf Kupfer, 40 × 30 cm

21 für Odilon – Zyklop (03.12.), 2009
   Öl auf Karton, 40 × 30 cm

41 Robinson (11.11.), 2009
   Öl auf Karton, 40 × 30 cm

43 Robinson (10.11.), 2009
   Öl auf Holz, 50 × 40 cm

45 Robinsons Albtraum (18.08.), 2009
   Öl auf Masonit, 60 × 45 cm

49 Hirsch (10.11.), 2009
   Öl auf Leinwand, 40 × 30 cm

50 St. Hubertus (18.11.), 2009
   Öl auf Karton, 40 × 30 cm

51 Frühling (01.03.), 2009
   Öl auf Karton, 30 × 24 cm

53 Bild (02.11.), 2008
   Öl auf Pappe, 40 × 30 cm

54 Bild (03.08.), 2009
   Öl auf Pappe, 35 × 25 cm

55 Wald (04.11.), 2009
   Öl auf Holz, 50 × 40 cm

57 für Caspar (01.07.), 2009
   Öl auf Leinwand, 50 × 40 cm

58 Nacht (12.12.), 2008
   Öl auf Holz, 40 × 30 cm

59 drei Hütten (07.01.), 2009
   Öl auf Holz, 40 × 30 cm

61 Diamond (03.06.), 2009
   Öl auf Karton, 50 × 40 cm

62 für Caspar (01.01.), 2009
   Öl auf Leinwand, 50 × 40 cm

63 Gold (03.07.), 2009
   Öl auf Holz, 30 × 21 cm

64 Bild (17.01.), 2009
   Öl auf Karton, 30 × 24 cm

65 Bild (06.08.), 2009
   Öl auf Holz, 40 × 30 cm

67 Bild (02.01.), 2009
   Öl auf Holz, 42 × 42 cm

71 abstrakt (07.10.), 2009
   Öl auf Holz, 60 × 40 cm

73 abstrakt (29.11.), 2009
   Öl auf Holz, 70 × 50 cm

75 abstrakt (16.12.), 2009
   Öl auf Holz, 60 × 50 cm

76 abstrakt (12.12.), 2009
   Öl auf Pappe, 41 × 30 cm

77 abstrakt (17.12.), 2009
   Öl auf Karton, 50 × 40 cm

79 abstrakt (26.12.), 2009
   Öl auf Holz, 45 × 35 cm

83 Tengu (09.11.), 2009
   Öl auf Karton, 30 × 40 cm

84 Tengu (05.12.), 2009
   Öl auf Kupfer, 25 × 20 cm

85 Tengu (06.12.), 2009
   Öl auf Zink, 25 × 20 cm

87 Tengu (13.11.), 2009
   Öl auf Karton, 30 × 40 cm

89 Tengu (10.11.), 2009
   Öl auf Pappe, 35.5 × 26.5 cm

91 Pinocchio (16.12.), 2009
   Öl auf Holz, 45 × 35 cm

Öl auf Holz / oil on wood
Öl auf Karton / oil on board
Öl auf Pappe / oil on cardboard
Öl auf Kupfer / oil on copper
Öl auf Masonit / oil on masonite
Öl auf Leinwand / oil on canvas
Öl auf Zink / oil on zinc

Einzelausstellungen
Solo exhibitions

Auswahl / **Selection**

2010 *new paintings*, Ancient & Modern, London (GB)
Norbert Prangenberg paintings, Betty
Cuningham Gallery, New York (USA), (Kat.) 2009
*Norbert Prangenberg: Esculturas, Pinturas
y Dibujos*, Galeria Manuel Ojeda,
Gran Canaria (ES)

2009 *die liebe farbe*, Galerie Rupert Walser, München
bilder Galerie Ebbers, Kranenburg

2008 *Neue Bilder*, Galerie Karsten Greve, Köln
*über und über – oder: wer malte den Mücken
die Flügel*, Kunstverein Lippstadt (Kat.)
Venustas et fortuna, Kunstmuseum Kloster
Unser Lieben Frauen, Magdeburg (Kat.)

2007 *Wasser zu Wein, Gold zu Stroh*,
Produzentengalerie Hamburg (Kat.)

2006 *Norbert Prangenberg. Malerei*, Museum
Katharinenhof, Kranenburg
Sculpture, Peinture, Dessin, Galerie Karsten
Greve, Paris (F)

2005 *Norbert Prangenberg. Zeichnungen 1978–2004*,
Staatliche Kunsthalle, Karlsruhe (Kat.)

2004 Norbert Prangenberg. Retrospektive der
Zeichnungen, Aquarelle, Gouachen 1978–2004,
Kaiser Wilhelm Museum, Krefeld (Kat.)
Skulpturen, Malerei, Zeichnungen,
Galerie Karsten Greve, Köln

2003 *Malerbücher-Norbert Prangenberg*,
Galerie Rupert Walser, München
Galerie Hollenbach, Stuttgart

2002 *Zeichnungen*, Barbara Gross Galerie, München
Skulpturen – Bilder – Zeichnungen,
Galerie Karsten Greve, Köln
Galerie Lisbeth Lipps, Rotterdam (NL)
Neue Arbeiten, Produzentengalerie Hamburg

2001 *Linolschnitte 1988–2001*, Städtische Galerie,
Bietigheim-Bissingen (Kat.)
Bayerische Versicherungskammer, München (Kat.)

2000 *Skulpturen auf dem Hermeshof –
Die Wurzel (Skulpturen und Zeichnungen)*,
Hermeshof, Rommerskirchen (Kat.)
Bilder & Skulpturen Galerie Hollenbach, Stuttgart
Malerei, Trinitatiskirche, Köln

1999 *Skulpturen*, Forum Rotunde Staatliche Kunsthalle,
Karlsruhe
Bilder und Aquarelle, Galerie Bismarck, Bremen
50.59 (mit Heinz Below), Zeche Zollverein Essen
Galerie Rupert Walser, München

1998 *Neue Bilder*, Barbara Gross Galerie, München
Galerie Karsten Greve Paris (F)
Produzentengalerie Hamburg
Galerie Harry Zellweger, Basel (CH)

1997 Europees Keramisch Werkcentrum,
s'Hertogenbosch (NL)

1996 Württembergischer Kunstverein, Stuttgart (Kat.)
Gemeentelijk Centrum voor Beeldende Kunst de
Beyerd, Breda (NL), (Kat.)
Westfälischer Kunstverein, Münster (Kat.)

1995 Kunstverein Ruhr, Essen (Kat.)
Galerie Bismarck, Bremen
Malerei, Barbara Gross Galerie, München

1994 *Bilder, Skulpturen, Aquarelle in der Sammlung
Finkenberg*, Neues Museum Weserburg, Bremen
Porcelaine de Sèvres, Galerie Karsten Greve,
Köln & Paris (F)
Galerie Tilly Haderek, Stuttgart
Produzentengalerie Hamburg

1993 *Bilder – Skulpturen – Zeichnungen*, Barbara Gross
Galerie, München

Gruppenausstellungen
Group exhibitions

Auswahl / **Selection**

Kunstverein, Heinsberg (Kat.)

Galerie Karsten Greve, Köln (mit Leiko Ikemura)

Krefelder Kunstverein, Krefeld

1992 *Morgenlandfahrer*, Galerie Karsten Greve, Köln

1991 *Bilder, Zeichnungen, Skulpturen*, Barbara Gross Galerie, München

Produzentengalerie Hamburg

1990 *N.P. Keramikskulpturen und Zeichnungen*, Badischer Kunstverein, Karlsruhe (Kat.)

Galerie Schneiderei, Köln

Galerie Karsten Greve, Paris (F)

1989 Kunstverein, Bochum

Plastische Arbeiten, Galerie Karsten Greve, Köln (Kat.)

Barbara Gross Galerie, München

Galerie Alexander Weder, Basel (CH)

1988 *Linolschnitte 1978-1988*, Kulturamt der Stadt Reutlingen (Kat.)

1987 *Bilder, Skulpturen, Zeichnungen*, Galerie Karsten Greve, Köln (Kat.)

Galerie Thomas Wallner, Malmö (S)

1986 *Norbert Prangenberg*, Gallery Hirschl & Adler, New York (USA) (Kat.)

Gesellschaft für Aktuelle Kunst, Bremen

1985 Knoedler Gallery, London (GB)

1984 Museum Haus Lange, Krefeld (Kat.)

Galerie Meyer-Ellinger, Frankfurt/M.

1983 Galerie Anders Tornberg, Lund (S)

Galerie Greve, Köln (Kat.)

Knoedler Gallery, London (GB)

1982 Bonner Kunstverein (mit Horst Münch), Bonn

1980 Galerie Karsten Greve, Köln

2010 *Aquarelle* Museum Liner, Appenzell (CH)

2009 *Die Gegenwart der Linie*, Staatl. Graphische Sammlung München

Der Holzschnitt im 20. & 21. Jh., Schatzhaus Spendhaus Reutlingen

2008 *3. Biennale der Zeichnung*, Kunstverein Esslingen

2007 *Als wäre nichts gesagt, Kunst der 80er Jahre aus den Sammlungen der Kunstmuseen Krefeld*, Museen Hans Lange, Haus Esters, Krefeld

Mandorla, 7hours, Haus 19, Berlin

slow food, Künstlerhaus Bethanien, Berlin

2006 *Painted in Munich*, Galerie Rupert Walser, München

2005 *Bilder vom Stein*, Pinakothek der Moderne, München

Bilanz in zwei Akten, Sammlung der Sparkassenstiftung, Kunstverein Hannover

2004 *Die welte Welt*, Graphische Sammlung, Museum Ludwig, Köln

2003 *Second World Ceramic Biennale* – CEBICO, Icheon World Ceramic Center, Icheon, Südkorea

2002 *Raum für Malerei/The Painting Room*, Kaiser-Wilhelm-Museum, Krefeld

Cologne Skulptur, Art Cologne, Köln

2001 *Ceramics*, Europäisches Patentamt München

AXA Art – Corporate Collecting Today, Köln

2000 *Sammlung Lauffs I*, Haus Lange, Krefeld

5 Positionen, Galerie Kraushaar, Düsseldorf

1999 *Die Kraft der Poesie*, PCC Kunstraum, Weimar

Schöpfung, Diözesanmuseum Freising

Ceramics by visitors, Frans Hals Museum, Haarlem (NL)

1998 *A ova expression de terra*, Coruna & Lugo (ES)

Leaf Spine, Word Sign, Künstlerbücher, Kunstmuseum, Bonn

1996 Skulpturenprojekt, Alden Biesen (BE)
Zeitströmungen – aus der Sammlung der Nieder-sächsischen Sparkassenstiftung, Hannover

1995 *Junge Kunst in Bremer Privatbesitz*, Gesellschaft für Aktuelle Kunst, Bremen
Das Abenteuer der Malerei, Kunstverein Stuttgart & Kunstverein, Düsseldorf

1991 *Drawn in the 90's*, Katonah Museum of Art, Katonah, New York (USA)
Kunst als Grenzüberschreitung: John Cage und die Moderne, Bayerische Staatsgemälde-sammlung, Neue Pinakothek, München

1990 *Klemm, Partenheimer, Prangenberg*, Goethe-Institut, London (GB) & Neue Pinakothek, München

1989 *Cologneer Kunst*, Kunstforeningen, Kopenhagen & Horsens Kunstmuseum Lunden (DK)

1988 *Mit Messer und Eisen... Holz- und Linolschnitte der Gegenwart*, Museum Schloss Morsbroich, Leverkusen

1987 *Wechselströme*, Bonner Kunstverein
Hans von Marees und die Moderne in Deutschland, Kunsthalle Bielefeld

1986 Biennal of Sydney, Sydney (AU)
Papier und Skulptur, Gesellschaft für aktuelle Kunst Bremen

1985 *Bremer Kunstpreis 1985*, Kunsthalle Bremen

1984 *Förderpreis des Landes Nordrhein-Westfalen*, Kunsthalle Bielefeld

1982 *documenta 7*, Kassel

1981 *Neue Sammlung (Prangenberg, Droese, Tannert, Christian)*, Museum Haus Esthers, Krefeld
Perspektive 1981 – Art 12 Basel (CH)

Norbert Prangenberg lebt und arbeitet in Niederarnbach und München

1949 geboren in Rommerskirchen, Rheinland
1963 Lehre als Gold- und Siberschmied
– 67 in Köln
1965 erste Holzschnitte und Zeichnungen
1976 erste Bilder und Skulpturen
1993 Professur an der Akademie der bildenden Künste München

Norbert Prangenberg lives and works in Niederarnbach and Munich

1949 born in Rommerskirchen, Rheinland
1963 appenticeship as gold- and silversmith
– 67 in Cologne
1965 first woodcuts and drawings
1976 first paintings and sculptures
1993 Professorship at the Academy of Fine Arts in Munich

Impressum
Imprint

Text
Walter Grasskamp, München

Übersetzung / Translation
Jacqueline Todd, Berlin

Korrektorat / Proofreading
Katrin Günther, Kerber Verlag, Leipzig (Deutsch / German)
Sarah Tolley, Edinburgh (Englisch / English)

Fotografie / Photography
Wilfried Petzi, München
Peter Sander, Hamburg (18, 19)

Bildbearbeitung / Picture editing
Joseph Sappler, Düsseldorf

Gestaltung / Graphic design
Bastian Ruppik, Düsseldorf

Gesamtherstellung / Printed and published by
Kerber Verlag, Bielefeld
Windelsbleicher Straße 166–170
D-33659 Bielefeld, Germany
Tel +49 (0) 5 21 9 50 08 10
Fax +49 (0) 5 21 9 50 08 88
info@kerberverlag.com
www.kerberverlag.com

Kerber, US Distribution
D.A.P., Distributed Art Publishers Inc.
155 Sixth Avenue 2nd Floor
New York, N.Y. 10013, USA
Tel +1 212 6 27 19 99
Fax +1 212 6 27 94 84

Titelabbildung / Cover illustration
Norbert Prangenberg,
nach einer Idee von Barbara Spaett

Die Deutsche Nationalbibliothek verzeichnet diese Publikation in der Deutschen
Nationalbibliografie; detaillierte bibliografische Daten sind im Internet über
http://dnb.ddb.de abrufbar. / The Deutsche Nationalbibliothek holds a record
of this publication in the Deutsche Nationalbibliografie; detailed bibliographical
data can be found under: http://dnb.ddb.de.

ISBN 978-3-86678-393-5

Printed in Germany

This catalogue is published on the occasion of the exhibition
Norbert Prangenberg – Paintings
Betty Cuningham Gallery, New York, April 1 – May 8, 2010
with special thanks to Bernd Schellhorn, Berlin

18 Exemplare dieses Kataloges erscheinen als limitierte Vorzugsausgabe,
signiert und nummeriert vom Künstler und enthalten je eine originale Tuscharbeit.

18 copies of this catalogue are published as a special limited edition,
signed & numbered by the artist, including an original ink drawing.